Made in Tanzania: Economics for Tanzanians

DAMAS MICHAEL MUSHI

DEDICATION

To Sr Philothea Mukure, Mary, Agnes and Michael

CONTENTS

ACKNOWLEDGMENTS

This book has been named "Made in Tanzania". Its subtitle is Economics for Tanzanians. Its contents introduce economics to beginners. Thanks to all students and colleagues who were a source of inspiration.

I acknowledge all people who have directly or indirectly contributed towards this work. My thanks go to my daughter and my son and my wife. My thanks go to my brothers and sisters. Also I thank my teachers and classmates and all family members who have contributed in my learning and teaching. Finally, the learning community in St Augustine University of Tanzania provided an enabling environment during the process of making the book. Thank you all for your love and understanding.

Damas Michael Mushi
February 2014

About the Book, the Students, and the Author

This book is an introduction to economics for beginners. The work is a contribution towards the advancement of economics education at secondary schools. The coverage is selective and an index is provided. Each chapter begins with a list of key terms which identifies the vocabulary a reader will need to learn in order to understand the material in the chapter. Learning objectives are bulleted so as to show the key points in the chapter. Each chapter ends with review questions. Beginners can use this book to supplement other relevant materials which are available and recommended by teachers. College students, undergraduate students and students in professional courses may also read the book and get useful information. Although this is a compact book with a limited space, a clear presentation makes it to be a recipe for revision. The contents and coverage are prim and precise. The author can be contacted through the following E-mail address: **damasmushi@ymail.com**

Published by Rock City Consultancy, P. O. Box 4019, Mwanza, Tanzania and CreateSpace Independent Publishers

Preface

"Made in Tanzania: Economics for Tanzanians" provides a concrete understanding of the basic economic concepts. It is a source of reflections during study. We know the feelings inherent whenever beginners approach economics subject. But, economics is a way of life and human beings are capable of understanding the workings of the economy. The book is also useful for the general public.

The contents of this book are formal and accurate. The contents have been tested, with a considerable academic success, in actual classroom settings. The author has been an education officer teaching economics subject in Tanzanian government secondary schools for more than six years.

Enjoy your reading as you participate in sharing the experience of the author who has been a student-teacher in economics for more than twenty five years. Again, this book is for beginners. Thus, the book is very selective in its coverage and depth of presentation. The expert guidance of experienced teachers is always desirable whenever using a book to complement main textbooks in schools. Why? The coverage and depth of presentation are selective! Students need guidance.

Damas Michael Mushi
February 2014.

███████████████████

Chapter One

What is economics?

KeyTerms	Objectives
Scarcity, economics, opportunity cost, goods, services, producer, consumer, production, exchange, distribution, consumption *Scarcity* is the condition that results from society not having enough resources to produce all the things people would like to have	In this chapter, you will ❑ define economics through the concept of scarcity ❑ understand why scarcity affects everyone ❑ learn three economic questions that society face because of scarcity ❑ understand the main economic activities ❑ understand the uses of the production possibilities curve

1.1   The Fundamental Economic Problem

The fundamental economic problem facing all societies is that of scarcity. But, what is scarcity? **Scarcity** is the condition that results from society not having enough resources to produce all the things people would like to have. Scarcity is a situation that exists because wants are unlimited and resources are limited. Unlimited consumer wants are greater than the quantity of factors of production available to produce goods and services. Goods and services are scarce. Consumers cannot satisfy all their wants and have to make a choice.

Any choice involves an opportunity cost. **Opportunity cost** is the real cost of making a choice; it is the best alternative choice which has been forgone. Opportunity cost is the cost of choice. Opportunity cost is the real cost of choosing one thing and not another.

Human choices, whether as individuals or communities, involve a conflict of interests. Why is it so? The reasoning is as follows: Scarce resources have alternative uses; and there is an opportunity cost. Not everyone can get what they want so some people will always be disappointed by the choices made by others.

1.2   A Definition of Economics

The fundamental economic problem suggests a working definition of economics. **Economics** is the study of how societies use scarce resources to produce valuable commodities and distribute them among different people. *Economics is the study of how people (individuals and societies) try to satisfy what appear to be seemingly unlimited and competing wants through the careful use of scarce resources.*

Economics involves:

1. Examining how individuals, businesses, governments, and societies choose to use scarce resources to satisfy their wants.
2. Organizing, analyzing, and interpreting data about those economic behaviours.
3. Developing theories and economic laws that explain how the economy works and to predict what might happen in the future.

1.3   Three Basic Questions

Because we live in a world of relative scarce resources, we have to make wise economic choices. Scarcity leads to three economic questions. The **three basic questions** we have to answer so as to make decisions about the ways our limited resources will be used are:
1.   What to produce? (What are we going to produce?)
2.   How to produce? (How is it to be produced?)
3.   For whom to produce? (Who receives how much?)

The three basic questions have to be answered in any economy. The questions have to be answered in all sectors of the economy.

An **economy** is an area in which people make, or produce goods and services. This area can be of any size, with any number of people involved. We can have a local economy involving a village or a city. We can have a global economy involving all countries together. In modern economy every individual is, somehow, a member in the global economy. For instance, at Nyamagana district people participate in both a local economy and a global economy. It all depends on the level of analysis for a particular economic activity.

The two main economic sectors are the private sector and the public sector. The **private sector** is made up of all the organizations and firms owned by members of the general public whether as private individuals or voluntary organizations. The **public sector** in an economy is owned and controlled by the government. Examples of the public sector are public education system, the armed forces, roads, and legal system.

1.4   The Main Economic Activities

The **key economic activities** that take place in all economies are as follows:
1. Production.
2. Consumption.
3. Exchange.
4. Distribution.

The circular flow of income is a model that can enable a person to grasp these four economic activities. The circular flow model is a tool for understanding the relationships among economic decision makers and various markets. For instance, the product market is the market where goods and services are bought and sold. On the other hand, the factor market is the market for the factors of production. Broadly, economic decision makers include:
1. Businesses (business firms);
2. Households (individuals);
3. Government;
4. Abroad (non-citizens)

Economic activities are done by the decision makers. The main types of economy have developed in attempts to solve the basic economic problem. The main types of economy are the market economy, the planned economy, and the mixed economy.

1.5   Scope of Economics

Let us remind ourselves that economics is the study of human effort to satisfy what appear to be unlimited and competing wants through the careful use of relatively scarce resources. There are four key elements in economics study.

The four key elements in economics study are:
1. Description.
2. Analysis.
3. Explanation.
4. Prediction.

Thus, the **scope of economics** is *the description, analysis, explanation, and prediction* of the key economic activities. Again, the key economic activities are production, consumption, exchange, and distribution.

1.6   Decision-Making

Decision-making is the process involving the following steps:
1. Define the problem.
2. List possible alternatives.
3. State criteria.
4. Use the criteria to evaluate each alternative.
5. Make a decision.

Behind all decision-making in economics there is the concept of opportunity cost.

1.7   Opportunity Cost

Wants are greater than resources. This means that goods and services are scarce. Therefore, consumers, for instance, have to make a choice. A choice involves an **opportunity cost**. Opportunity cost is the best alternative choice which has been forgone.

Choice is at the heart of economics. "There is no such thing as a free lunch." This adage describes the concept of opportunity cost. The production possibilities frontier can be used to illustrate the concept of the opportunity cost.

1.8   Goods and Services

What do resources produce?   Resources may produce consumer goods and services, capital goods, public goods and merit goods.   A producer is a maker of goods and provider of services.   A consumer is a user of goods and services.   Consumption is the process of consumers using goods and services because it gives them satisfaction. Consumer goods are those goods produced to give immediate satisfaction to consumers, for example food and videos.   Durable goods are those consumer goods which have a relatively long life, for example, motor-cars, videos and sofa sets.

1.9   The Production-Possibilities Frontier

The **production-possibilities frontier** (PPF) model, also called production possibilities curve (PPC) is a model which shows the maximum amounts of production that can be obtained by the economy, given its technological knowledge and quantity of inputs available.   The PPF represents the menu of goods and services available to society. The PPC is the graph used by economists to show the impact of scarcity on an economy. We note that an economic model is a simplified representation of economic forces.   The PPC is based on the assumptions that simplify the economic interactions.

For the PPC these assumptions are:
1. Resources are fixed.
2. All resources are fully employed.
3. Only two things can be produced.
4. Technology is fixed.

There are many uses of the PPC. The PPC can be used to illustrate:
*   Impact of scarcity.
*   Efficiency.
*   Underutilization.
*   Law of increasing costs.
*   Changing production possibilities.

Thus, the PPC as a graph used by economists to show the impact of scarcity can also illustrate other economic concepts. Here, efficiency involves producing the amount of goods and services possible. Efficiency is attained along the PPC curve. Underutilization means producing fewer goods and services than possible. The "law of increasing costs" states that as production switches from one product to another, increasing amounts of resources are needed to increase the production of the second product.

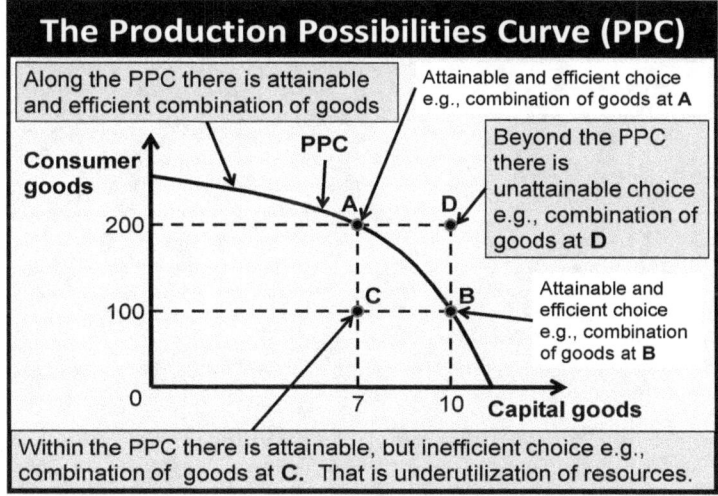

The Production Possibilities Curve (PPC)

Along the PPC there is attainable and efficient combination of goods

Attainable and efficient choice e.g., combination of goods at **A**

Beyond the PPC there is unattainable choice e.g., combination of goods at **D**

Attainable and efficient choice e.g., combination of goods at **B**

Within the PPC there is attainable, but inefficient choice e.g., combination of goods at **C**. That is underutilization of resources.

Whenever the assumptions used to sketch the original PPC are relaxed, the PPC shifts. For instance when there is either an improvement in technology or an increase in resources the PPC may shift and bulge outwards. That shift shows an economic growth. The diagram of the PPC to show economic growth is provided below.

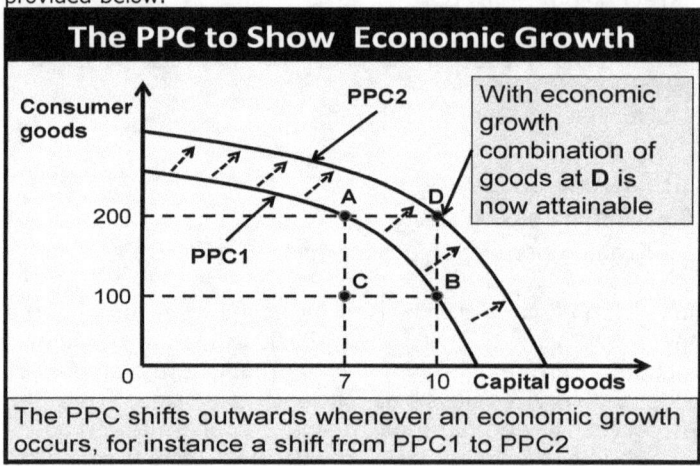

The PPC to Show Economic Growth

The PPC shifts outwards whenever an economic growth occurs, for instance a shift from PPC1 to PPC2

Review Questions

1. "Scarcity and choice are like the two sides of the same coin. They are intrinsically related." Comment.
2. "The production possibilities frontier has many uses." Discuss.
3. "There is no such thing as a free lunch." How far is the concept of an opportunity cost related to this proverb?
4. Mention the four key economic activities.
5. Discuss the scope of economics.
6. What are the three basic questions that have to be answered in any economy?
7. What is the fundamental economic problem?
8. What is economics?

Chapter Two

Economic Systems

Key Terms	Objectives
Economic systems, command economy, market economy, mixed economy *An economic system* is the way in which a society uses its scarce resources to satisfy its people's unlimited wants	In this chapter, you will ❏ define an economic system ❏ explain the advantages and disadvantages of command economies and market economies ❏ understand why most modern economies are mixed economies ❏ identify criteria for evaluating economic performance

2.1   An Economy

An **economy** (economic system) is an organized way of providing for the wants and needs of people in the society. The ways in which these provisions are made determines the type of economic system in the society. In other words, an economic system is the way in which a society uses its scarce resources to satisfy its people's unlimited wants. An economy is an area in which people make, or produce, goods and services. Economists across the world agree that the basic economic problem is that of scarcity of resources. All other economic problems derive from this. It is this problem which all economic systems attempt to overcome.

Major Kinds of Economic Systems

Leaving aside a society with a traditional economy whereby the allocation of scarce resources, and nearly all other economic activity stems from ritual, habit, or custom, the three major kinds of economic systems are:
1. Market economies.
2. Planned economies.
3. Mixed economies.

2.2   The Market Economy System

A **market economy** is an economic system in which an individual choice and voluntary exchange direct economic decisions. In a market economy, people and firms act in their own best interests to answer the "what", "how", and "for whom" questions. Thus, a market economy is an economic system based on individual choice, voluntary exchange, and the private ownership of resources.

A **market** is an arrangement that allows buyers and sellers to come together in order to exchange goods and services. In a market economy, people's decisions act as votes. There are various other terms for the market economy such as the capitalist economy, the 'laissez-faire' economy, and the private enterprise economy. In the market economy scarce resources are allocated without any government interference. The market decides what will be produced.

Fundamentals of a Market Economy

Market economies have the following distinct characteristics:
1. Private property and markets.
2. Limited government involvement.
3. Voluntary exchange in markets.
4. Competition and consumer sovereignty.
5. Specialization.

Advantages of the Market Economy

Advantages of the market economy include the following:
1. There is minimal state interference.
2. There is consumer sovereignty.
3. There is a wide variety of different goods and services to meet consumer's wants.
4. Resources are allocated efficiently.
5. The free market responds quickly to people's wants.
6. Competition leads to low prices for consumers.
7. The market system encourages the use of new and better methods and machines to produce goods and services.
8. Economic freedom coexists with political freedom for consumers.

The advantages of the market economy are the hints on how good is the market economic system.

Disadvantages of the Market Economy

Disadvantages of the market economy include the following:
1. Unprofitable goods are not produced by private enterprises, that is, factors of production will be employed only if it is profitable to do so.
2. The free market can fail to provide certain goods and services.
3. The free market may encourage the consumption of harmful goods.
4. The social effects of production may be ignored.
5. Market economy may allow an inevitable inequality in income and wealth distribution.
6. The market system allocates more goods and services to those consumers who have more money than others.
7. Scarce resources may be allocated to produce luxury commodities.
8. Few or a single individual may dominate industries.
9. The market system is prone to trade cycles.

The disadvantages of the market system are the hints on what may be wrong with the market system.

2.3   The Planned Economy System

A **planned economy** is one in which a central authority makes most of what, how, and for whom decisions. Economic decisions are made by the government. The people have little influence over how the basic economic questions are answered. Other names for the planned economy are: the command economy, the collective economy, and the communist economy. In a planned economy system scarce resources are allocated by the government. State planners decide what will be produced, where and how.

Advantages of the Planned Economy System

Advantages of the planned economy system include the following:
1. A more equal distribution of income and wealth.
2. Unprofitable goods may be provided.
3. Scarce resources can be allocated to the production of the necessities such as basic foodstuffs.
4. A smooth reallocation of resources.
5. The wastes and duplications of the market economy can be avoided.
6. Private monopolists will not exist.

Disadvantages of the Planned Economy System

Disadvantages of the planned economic system include the following:
1. Planners may make wrong decisions.
2. Workers and managers may have no incentive to work hard.
3. Many bureaucrats are needed to run the system.
4. Government decides what a luxury is and what a necessity is.

2.4   The Mixed Economy System

The **mixed economy** system includes aspects of both the market system and the planned system. To some extent all economies are mixed, differing only in the degree of market and planning involved. Because of the disadvantages of both market and planned economic systems most countries in the world choose to use a mixed economic system. The mixed economic system combines government planning with the use of free market.

A mixed economy attempts to overcome the disadvantages of a market economic system by using government intervention to control or regulate different markets. Thus, most modern economies are mixed economies. Tanzania has a mixed economy system. The same applies to Kenya, Uganda, Burundi and Rwanda.

2.5   Evaluating Economic Performance

A mixed economy such as that which is found in Tanzania has **economic and social goals** which can be used to evaluate its performance. Economic performance, for instance in Tanzania, can be evaluated according to the following criteria:
1. Economic freedom (freedom of choice).
2. Economic efficiency.
3. Economic equity. A fair distribution of national income.
4. Full employment.
5. Price stability. A generally stable level of prices.
6. Economic growth. A continually rising level of real incomes.
7. Equality between the values of what we sell to other countries and what we buy from them.
8. Tanzanian ownership of its industries.

There may be trade-offs among the goals.

Review Questions

1. What is an economic system?
2. Mention the major kinds of economic systems.
3. Discuss the advantages and disadvantages of the following economic systems:
   a) Market economies
   b) Planned economies.
4. "All economic systems attempt to overcome the basic economic problem (of scarcity)." Discuss.
5. Mention the distinct characteristics of market economies.
6. "Tanzania has a mixed economy." Discuss.
7. Mention the economic and social goals that may be used to evaluate the performance of an economy.

Chapter Three

Production and Economic Growth

Key Terms	Objectives
Production, economic growth, specialization, economies of scale, diseconomies of scale, Gross Domestic Product	In this chapter, you will
	❑ define production
Production is the creation of goods and services which consumers are prepared to consume so as to satisfy their wants	❑ understand the advantages and disadvantages of large scale production
	❑ account for the survival of small firms
Economic growth represents the expansion of a country's potential GDP	❑ provide a meaning of economic growth and describe its determinants
	❑ identify the benefits and costs of economic growth

3.1   Meaning of Production

Production is the process of creating goods and services. The production process involves the use of factors of production so as to create goods and services which consumers are prepared to consume so as to satisfy their wants.   Production is not finished until the goods and services are in the hands of the final consumer.   Production creates utility and value.

Where does production take place? Production takes place in a firm, a plant and an industry. A **firm** is an organization that turns factors of production into outputs of goods and services. A **plant** is a work place. It is a unit of production. An **industry** consists of all the firms in an economy producing very similar goods and services for a particular market.

The Factors of Production

The quality and quantity of factors of production depends on the quality and quantity of available resources. The **factors of production** are the resources required to produce the things we would like to have. The factors of production are the inputs into the production process from which an output of goods and services emerges. The four factors of production that are required if goods and services are to be produced are:
1. Labor.
2. Land.
3. Capital.
4. Enterprise.

Labour is the mental and physical human effort involved in the production process. Labour is human resources. Labour earns an income or reward which is called wages.
Land includes all kinds of natural resources such as farmland, raw material deposits, and climate, forest and fishing grounds. Land is natural resources. Owners of land earn a reward or income which is called rent.
Capital comprises all those resources required not for their own sakes but because they produce other commodities.

Examples of capital include factory premises, machinery, and raw materials in stock, transport vehicles, and partly finished goods. Producer goods (also known as capital goods) are those goods produced to produce other goods and services, for example machinery and factories. Capital is man-made resources which help to produce many other goods and services. Owners of capital earn a reward or income which is called interest.

Enterprise (entrepreneurship) is business know-how which is the ability to run a production process. Enterprise is the factor of production which brings together the other three. The entrepreneur is the organizer who decides what to be produced, where and how. The entrepreneur carries the risks of production in a firm. The reward for successful decisions of the entrepreneur is a profit.

Types of Production (Stages of Production)

There are broadly speaking, three categories of activities involved in the process of production. These categories are also called stages of production. They are:

1. Primary production (primary industry).
2. Secondary production (secondary industry).
3. Tertiary production (tertiary industry).

Primary production is the first stage in the production process. It includes all those industries engaged in extracting raw materials, farming, forestry, and fishing. The products of those industries are used by industries involved in secondary production.

Secondary production includes all those industries involved in manufacturing the finished goods using the raw materials provided by primary industries. Examples include steel, baking and brewing.

Tertiary production includes all those industries which provide the services which are necessary for the production to take place.

There are two types of services namely personal services and commercial services. Examples of personal services are the services provided by doctors, dentists, and teachers to persons. Examples of commercial services are banking, accountancy, and advertising services to the industry. Commercial services ensure that the finished good reaches the consumer at the right time, in the right place, and in the right quantity and quality. There is a tendency for a growth of tertiary production in the modern developed economy.

3.2   The Division of Labour and Specialization

In the modern economy factors of production tend to specialize in certain types of production. In the context of labour, **division of labour** occurs when the production process is divided up so that an individual undertakes only a small part of the total work. The main advantages of division of labour are that production is increased and the costs per unit of output are reduced. Division of labour requires exchange. Division of labour is limited by the size of the market.

Determinants of the Extent of Division of Labour

Determinants of the extent of division of labour include:
1. Size of the firm.
2. Level of technology.
3. Number of labour.
4. Size of the market.

Types (Forms) of Division of Labour

Types (forms) of division of labour include:
1. Division of labour by process.
2. Division of labour by sex.
3. Division of labour by age.
4. Division of labour by territory or country.
5. Division of labour by product/region.
6. Division of labour by profession (particular training or skills).

Advantages of Division of Labour

Advantages of division of labour include the following:
1. An increase in production. More goods and services are produced.
2. A reduction in costs per unit of output.
3. Time is saved.
4. More economic use of tools and machines.
5. Workers develop skills while doing repetitive tasks. Practice makes perfect.
6. Workers can specialize in a job in which they have some ability. Full use is made of everyone's ability.
7. Machinery can be developed to replace that labour doing the most basic repetitive tasks.
8. Division of labour may develop into mass production.

Disadvantages of Division of Labour

Disadvantages of division of labour include the following:
1. Repetitive tasks are boring and tiresome.
2. Workers may feel alienated from fellow-workers and managers.
3. A loss of traditional skills and craftsmanship.
4. All workers are interdependent and if disruption occurs in one part of the production process, then the whole process may be brought to a halt. People become too dependent upon each other.
5. There is a lack of variety of commodities which are produced. Products are all the same.

3.3   Large-Scale Production

The **scale of production** refers to the quantity produced and the technique used in production. Large scale means a greater quantity is produced by a particular firm in an industry, while small scale means a small quantity is produced by a particular firm in an industry.
The scale of production depends on the following factors:
1. Availability of resources (capital and labour).
2. Size of the market.
3. Technological level.
4. Availability of infrastructures.

The Economies of Large-Scale Production

The **economies of large scale production** may be due to internal economies of scale and external economies of scale. **Internal economies** of scale are the advantages obtained by *a single* firm when it expands the size of production.
Internal economies of scale include:
1. Financial economies.
2. Marketing economies.
3. Economies in bulk buying.
4. Economies in decreasing average cost.
5. Technical economies.
6. Economies in administration.
7. Economies in the use of factors of production.
8. Research economies.

External economies of scale are advantages which are obtained by *all firms* in a particular industry due to localization. Localization is the concentration of many firms in one area.
External economies of scale include:
1. Infrastructural facilities.
2. Availability of factors of production.
3. Decrease in the cost of production.
4. Regional division of labour.

The Diseconomies of Large-Scale Production

The **diseconomies of scale** are the disadvantages that a firm experience when it expands the scale of production.
The diseconomies of scale include:
1. Increase in cost.

2. Difficulty in controlling production.
3. Difficulty in management and control of labour.
4. Marketing diseconomies
5. Technical diseconomies.
6. Diseconomies of division of labour.
7. Diseconomies of standardized products.
8. Diseconomies of bureaucratic control.
9. Financial diseconomies.

3.4   Survival of Small Firms

Why are there small firms? There are some reasons why small firms still exist. When economists account for the **survival of small firms** the possible reasons include:

1. The size of the market may be small, that is, small extent of the market.
2. A wide variety of goods and services are wanted.
3. Luxury items are highly priced.
4. Direct contact with customers (people like personal services).
5. Small scale firms supply inputs to large scale firms (a large firm requires component parts).
6. Small firms require small initial and running capital.
7. Government assistance to small firms.
8. Personal choice of entrepreneurs to operate a small firm.

3.5   Economic Growth

What is economic growth? **Economic growth** occurs whenever the total amount of goods and services (or real output) an economy can produce increases over time.

As a result of economic growth, the national income will grow in real terms. Thus, economic growth represents the expansion of a country's potential GDP (Gross Domestic Product) or national output. Here we mention the factors for economic growth. Then, we identify the possible benefits and costs of economic growth.

Factors for Economic Growth

The following are the ways (factors) in which economic growth can be achieved:
1. Natural resources (land, minerals, fuels, environmental quality, the discovery of more natural resources).
2. Capital formation (investment in capital such as, machines, factories, roads).
3. Technology (technical progress such as science, engineering, management, entrepreneurship).
4. Human resources (labour supply, education, discipline, motivation, i.e., increasing in the amount and quality of human services).

The factors for economic growth are also called the four wheels of economic growth.

The Benefits of Economic Growth

The benefits of economic growth include the following:
1. Higher levels of consumption for all to enjoy, providing they have money to buy these goods.
2. Higher level of output.
3. Rising income.

Costs of Economic Growth

The costs of economic growth may include the following:
1. An opportunity cost of growth.
2. Scarce resources may be used up more quickly.
3. Pollution.
4. Unemployment.

Review Questions

1. What is production? Mention the four factors of production and the respective rewards to each factor.
2. Outline the advantages of division of labour.
3. Outline the disadvantages of division of labour.
4. Mention the three categories of activities which are involved in the process of production.
5. Mention the advantages of large scale production.
6. Mention the disadvantages of large scale production.
7. Account for the survival of small firms.
8. What is economic growth? Mention the four wheels of economic growth.
9. Discuss the benefits and costs of economic growth.

Chapter Four

Business Organizations

Key Terms	Objectives
Business organization, sole proprietorship, partnerships, corporations, co-operatives, government organizations, public sector, private sector, nationalization, privatization	In this chapter, you will
	❏ define a business organization
	❏ state the advantages and disadvantages of the various types of business organizations
A business is any person or group of people which sells goods or services which keep people alive or make life more enjoyable	❏ explain the difference between a public sector business and a private sector business
	❏ provide arguments for and against nationalization
	❏ provide arguments for and against privatization

4.1   Forms of Business Organizations

A **business organization** is any person or group of people which sells goods or services which keep people alive or make life more enjoyable.   There are various types of business organizations. The main forms (types) of business organizations in the economy today are:

1. Sole proprietorships.
2. Partnerships.
3. Corporations.

4. Community and civic organizations.
5. Cooperatives.
6. Labour, professional, and business organizations.
7. Government.

Single Ownership

The **sole proprietor** (single owner) owns the entire business; controls the decision making; receives all the profits; is responsible for all the debts; raises money from his own capital, retained profit and borrowing; and possible aims are to make a profit, grow larger, keep control, security and independence.

Advantages of the sole trader are as follows:
1. The sole trader business is a very personal one.
2. The sole trader is his/her own boss.
3. The sole trader receives all the profits.
4. It is easy to set up a sole trader business.

Disadvantages of the sole trader are as follows:
1. The sole trader has unlimited liability.
2. The sole trader has full responsibility.
3. Sole trader may lack capital.

Partnership

A **partnership** consists of between two and twenty people who jointly own a business and work in it together.

Advantages of partnership include the following:
1. Partners bring new skills and ideas to a business.
2. More partners mean more money for the business.
3. Partners can help in decision making.

Disadvantages of partnerships include the following:
1. Partners can disagree.
2. Some partners may have joint unlimited liability.
3. Partnerships may lack capital.

Corporations

Corporations are companies which may be private limited companies or public limited companies.
Advantages of the *private limited company:*
1. Shareholders have limited liability.
2. Shareholders have no management worries.
3. The company has a separate legal entity.

Disadvantages of *private limited companies:*
1. Limited companies must disclose information about themselves to the general public.
2. Limited companies must hold an annual general meeting (AGM) of shareholders each year.
3. The original owners of the company may lose control.
4. Company profits are taxed twice.
5. Private limited companies cannot sell shares on the stock market.

Advantages of the *public limited companies:*
1. Public limited companies can sell shares publicly.
2. Public limited companies can publicly advertise their shares.

Disadvantages of the *public limited companies:*
1. It can be expensive to form a public limited company.
2. There is divorce of ownership from control.
3. There are management diseconomies.

Co-operatives

Co-operatives are business organizations that are owned and controlled by a group of people, to undertake an economic activity to their mutual benefit. The two main types of co-operatives are:
1. Worker co-operatives.
2. Consumer co-operatives.

Public Enterprise

Public sector organizations are those owned and controlled by government. The four main types of government organizations are:
1. Central government.
2. Local government.
3. Government agencies.
4. Public corporations.

4.2 Public Sector versus Private Sector

There are two basic types of business ownership namely the private sector and the public sector. The private sector includes all businesses owned by individuals, either in their own or in groups. In the private sector the owners set the objectives of the business.

Businesses in the public sector are owned by the State or by local authorities. The objectives of these businesses are set by the government or the local council for the benefit of the whole community.

Private Sector Objectives

The objectives of private sector businesses may include:
1. Making profit.
2. Survival.
3. Having a good public image.
4. Growing larger.
5. Increasing sales.

Usually, the main aim of private sector businesses is to make profits for its owner or owners. Whenever other aims are considered, the profit motive is always at the background because in the long-run, without external assistance, it is impossible for a private sector firm to carry on with losses.

Public Sector Objectives

The objectives of publicly owned businesses emphasize the good of the whole community. The community is supreme.

A Growing Interest in the Ownership of Businesses

Economists are interested on how a business is owned for a variety of reasons. How a business is owned affects aspects such as the way in which it is financed; who makes the decisions, that is, who controls the business; who is responsible for the actions of the business?; and, the goals of the business. These aspects help in understanding the behavior of the business entities and the way they interact with each in an economy.

4.3   Nationalization

What is nationalization? **Nationalization** is the process of transferring private owned property and business to the state.   To nationalize means to change from private ownership to government or public ownership.

Arguments in Favour of Nationalization

Arguments in favour of nationalization include the following issues:

1. To achieve economies of large-scale production.
2. The "commanding heights of the economy" argument.
3. To avoid private monopolies.
4. Certain industries are operated better when organized on a national basis.
5. It may be unwise from the point of view of national security for certain industries to be in the hands of private enterprise.
6. Where much capital is needed it may be better to have nationalization.
7. Social consideration.
8. Political consideration.

Arguments against Nationalization

Arguments against nationalization include the following issues:
1. Political consideration.
2. Nationalized industries suffer from the diseconomies of large-scale production.
3. There is lack of profit motive which results in inefficiency and loss-making.

4. There is too much political interference.
5. Nationalized industries form state or public monopolies.
6. Public accountability may be questionable.

4.4   Privatization

What is privatization? **Privatization** is the process of transferring state owned property and business to individuals. To privatize means to change from government or public ownership to private ownership.

Arguments for Privatization

Arguments for privatization include the following issues:
1. When nationalized industries are returned to competitive market condition and are driven by profit motive, there will be more efficiency, and destruction of public monopolies.
2. In privatization, management is freed from government interference in decision making.
3. Privatization may make possible the raising of more finance from private sector.
4. In privatization, the financial burden on the government is reduced.
5. In privatization, the market mechanism is allowed to operate more freely to allocate resources.

Arguments against Privatization

Arguments against privatization include the following
issues:
1. In privatization, public monopolies are merely replaced by private monopolies.
2. Returning nationalized industries to private enterprise may mean more unemployment as the industry is driven only by the profit motive.
3. In privatization, only the profitable parts of the public sector will successfully be sold to private enterprise.
4. Nationalized industries may be sold too cheaply, allowing private investors large capital gains.

Review Questions

1. Mention the main forms of business organization.
2. What are the possible advantages of a sole proprietor?
3. What are the possible disadvantages of a sole proprietor?
4. Provide a list of at least five possible objectives of a private sector business organization.
5. Distinguish between nationalization and privatization.
6. Provide arguments for and against nationalization.
7. Provide arguments for and against privatization.

Chapter Five

Supply, Demand and the Market

Supply, Demand and the Market

Key Terms	Objectives
Equilibrium price, equilibrium quantity, supply, demand, supply schedule, demand schedule, supply curve, demand curve, change in supply, change in quantity supplied, change in demand, change in quantity demanded, market	In this chapter, you will
	❑ understand the distinction between schedules and curves
	❑ define supply and outline what the law of supply says
	❑ define demand and outline what the law of demand says
The equilibrium price is the price at which quantity demanded and quantity supplied are the same	❑ explain how supply and demand may determine price in a free market economy
	❑ identify the roles of price in a free market economy

5.1   Supply

Supply is the desire and ability to produce and sell a product.   The law of supply states that other things remaining the same, there is a direct relationship between the quantity supplied of a commodity and its price.   Thus, sellers would tend to supply more at a higher price than at a lower price, other factors remaining constant.

Supply Schedules

Supply schedule is a listing of how much of an item an individual is willing to sell at each price.

An Individual Supply Schedule	
Price of oranges (in Tshs per orange)	Quantity of oranges supplied per week
10	4
20	5
30	6
40	7
50	8
60	9
70	10

Market supply schedule is a listing of how much of an item all suppliers are willing to sell at each price. [If we assume that there are ten equal suppliers in the market, then we have the following market supply schedule].

An Market Supply Schedule	
Price of oranges (in Tshs per orange)	Quantity of oranges supplied per week
10	40
20	50
30	60
40	70
50	80
60	90
70	100

The data contained in the market supply schedule can be used to plot a market supply curve.

Supply Curves

A **supply curve** shows the data from a supply schedule in a graph form. A market supply curve shows the data from a market supply schedule in graph form. The supply curve, derived from the supply schedule, is a graphical representation of the total quantities which all suppliers together are prepared to offer for sale over a range of prices. The shape of the supply curve is upward slopping from left to right. Firms are prepared to offer more of a commodity for sale at higher prices because they are able to earn higher profits by doing so.

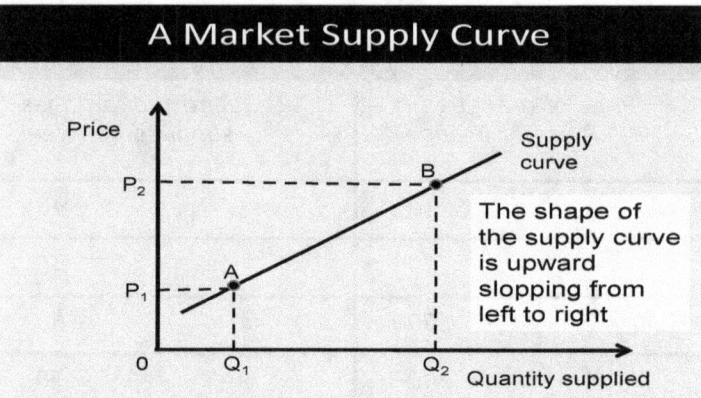

All points on or above the supply curve are attainable, and those below the supply curve are non-attainable.

The major factors which determine supply are: the price of the commodity; the prices of factors of production; and, the methods of production.

Determinants of Quantity Supplied

Factors which may influence quantity supplied in market are as follows:
1. Price of the commodity.
2. Price of other related commodities (for instance competing commodities and commodities which are produced together).
3. Prices and availability of factors of production.
4. Expectations about the future prices of goods.
5. Goals of firms.
6. State of technology.
7. Weather and climate.
8. Government policy (on taxes and subsidies).

9. Number of producers.
10. Freedom of entry and exit.
11. Demand.
12. Gestation period.
13. Political situation.
14. Working conditions.

The above mentioned factors are the determinants of market supply.

Movement On or Along the Supply Curve

Movement on or along the supply curve is also called **change in quantity supplied**. When the price increases, the quantity supplied also expands along the supply curve. That is called an extension of supply. On the other hand, when the price falls, the quantity supplied contracts along the supply curve. That is called a contraction of supply

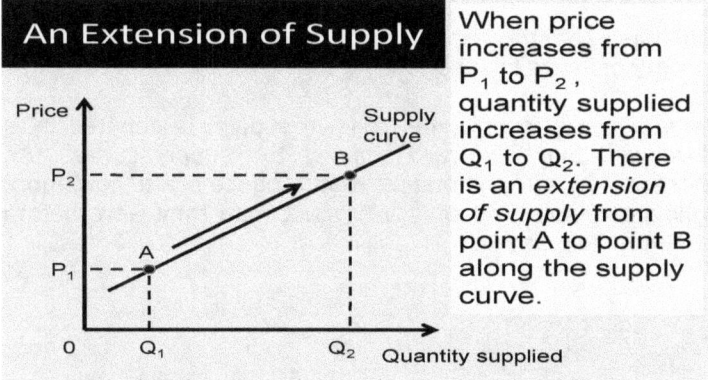

An Extension of Supply

When price increases from P_1 to P_2, quantity supplied increases from Q_1 to Q_2. There is an *extension of supply* from point A to point B along the supply curve.

An **extension of supply** refers to how supply changes with a rise in the price of a product, given that no other factor affecting supply changes.

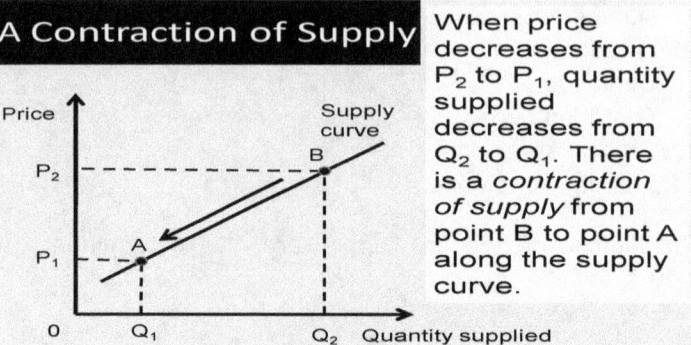

When price decreases from P_2 to P_1, quantity supplied decreases from Q_2 to Q_1. There is a *contraction of supply* from point B to point A along the supply curve.

A **contraction of supply** refers to how supply changes with a fall in the price of a product, without a change in any other factor that may affect supply. Note that the change in quantity supplied is a rise or fall in the amount that producers offer for sale because of a change in price.

Movement off the Supply Curve

Movement off the supply curve is also called **changes in supply** or shifts in supply.

An increase in supply, i.e., rise in supply, is denoted by a downward and rightward shift of the supply curve. An **increase in supply** means that producers are now more willing and able to supply a product than they were before at all possible prices.

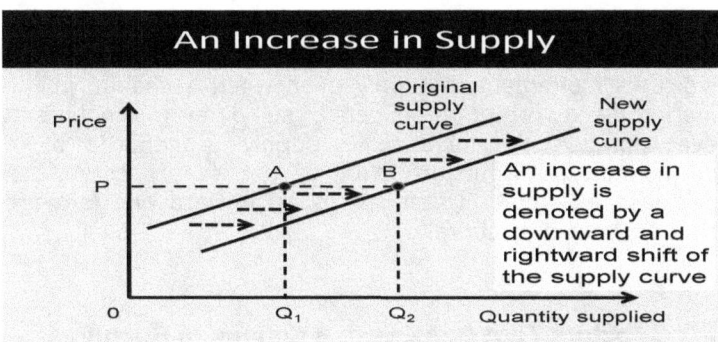

A decrease in supply, i.e., fall in supply, is denoted by an upward and leftward shift of the supply curve. A **fall in supply** means that producers are now less willing and able to supply a product at each and every price than they were before at all possible prices.

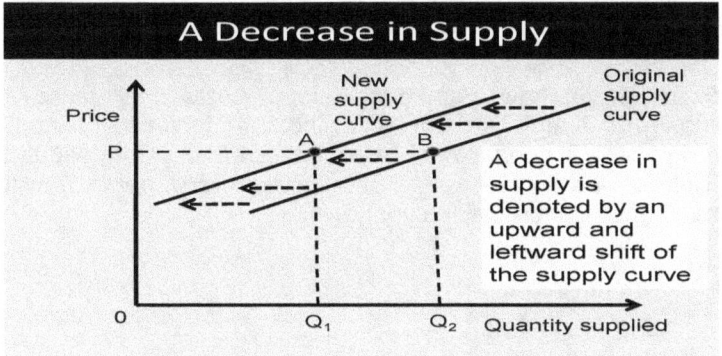

Increase or decrease in the supply for a good refers to movement of the quantity supplied off the supply curve. It indicates movement in supply even when a change in the market place prompts producers to sell different amounts at every price. An increase in supply is denoted by a downward and rightward shift of the supply curve. A decrease in supply is denoted by an upward and leftward shift of the supply curve.

Factors That Can Cause a Change in Supply

Factors that can cause a change in supply are as follows:
1. A change in input costs.
2. A change in labour productivity.
3. A change in technology.
4. A change in government action (for instance with reference to taxes and subsidies)
5. A change in producer expectations
6. A change in the number of producers.

Examples on how a change in input costs may cause a change in supply are the following: A decrease in input costs, *ceteris paribus*, will result into an increase in supply. Likewise, an increase in input costs, *ceteris paribus*, will result into a decrease in supply.

5.2   Demand

Demand is the willingness to buy a good or service and the ability to pay for it. The law of demand states that other things remaining the same, the quantity demanded of a commodity is inversely related to its price. Buyers will reduce their purchases of a commodity when its price rises and will increase their purchases if the price falls. Thus, other things being equal, more of a commodity is bought when its price is lower and less of it is bought when its price is higher.

Demand Schedules

Demand schedule is a listing of how much an item an individual is willing to purchase at each price.

An Individual Demand Schedule	
Price of oranges (in Tshs per orange)	Quantity of oranges supplied per week
10	10
20	9
30	8
40	7
50	6
60	5
70	4

Market demand schedule is a listing of how much an item all consumers are willing to purchase at each price. [If we assume that there are ten equal consumers (demanders/buyers) in the market, then we have the following demand schedule.]

An Market Demand Schedule	
Price of oranges (in Tshs per orange)	Quantity of oranges supplied per week
10	100
20	90
30	80
40	70
50	60
60	50
70	40

The data contained in the market demand schedule can be used to plot a market demand curve.

Demand Curves

The graphical representation of the market demand schedule is called the market demand curve. The **demand curve** shows, in the form of a graph, the quantities demanded by consumers of the same product over a range of prices. The normal shape of the demand curve is downward sloping from left to right. The slope of the curve is from left to right showing that more of a commodity is demanded as the price falls.

44

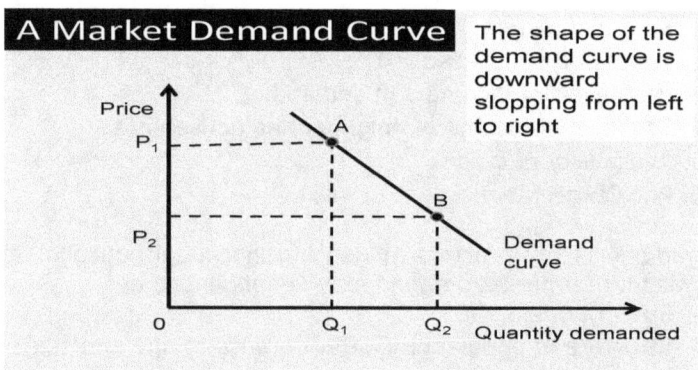

Any point lying above the demand curve is not attainable, while any point lying on or below the demand curve is attainable.

The major factors which determine the level of demand for any commodity include:

1. Price of the commodity.
2. Income of consumers.
3. The personal taste of consumers.
4. The prices of other commodities.
5. Complementary commodities.
6. Substitutes.

Determinants of Quantity demanded

Factors that influence individual household demand may include:

1. Price of the commodity.
2. Prices of other commodities (substitutes and complements).
3. Income of an individual.
4. Expectation about future income.
5. Tastes and preferences.

6. Seasonal factors.
7. Taxes and subsidies.
8. Past levels of income and demand.
9. The level of income of neighbouring households.
10. Availability of credit.
11. Price expectations.

In addition to the factors influencing individual households' demand, the market demand may be influenced by:
1. Size of population.
2. Structure of population (with reference to age and sex).
3. Income distribution among households.
4. Government expenditure.
5. Money supply.
6. Exchange rate.

The above mentioned factors are the determinant of market demand.

Movement On or Along the Demand Curve

Movement on or along the demand curve is also called a **change in quantity demanded**. Change in quantity demanded is an increase or decrease in the amount demanded because of change in price.

For instance, in response to a fall in the price, the quantity demanded of the good expands. That is called an extension of demand. On the other hand, a rise in price leads to a fall in the quantity demanded. That is called a contraction of demand.

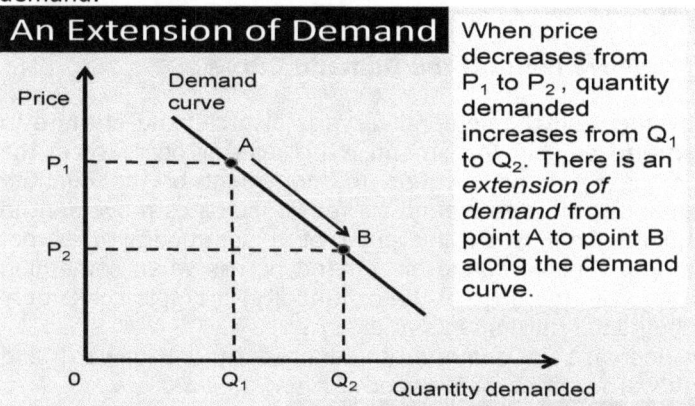

An Extension of Demand

When price decreases from P_1 to P_2, quantity demanded increases from Q_1 to Q_2. There is an *extension of demand* from point A to point B along the demand curve.

An **extension of demand** or increase in quantity demanded refers to the way in which demand changes with a fall in price, with no change in any other factor that could affect demand.

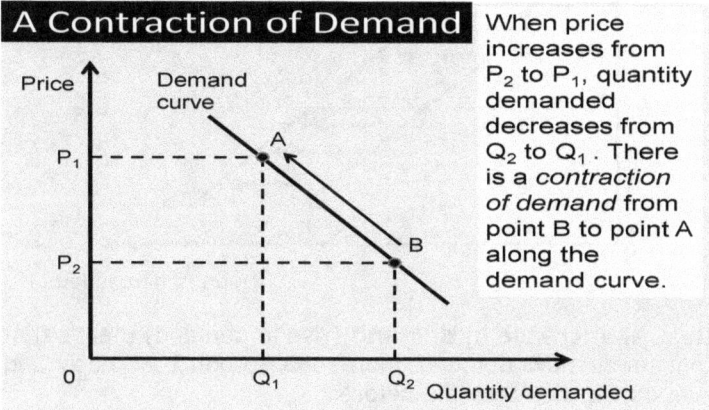

A Contraction of Demand

When price increases from P_2 to P_1, quantity demanded decreases from Q_2 to Q_1. There is a *contraction of demand* from point B to point A along the demand curve.

A **contraction of demand** or decrease in quantity demanded refers to the way in which demand changes when price rises, with no change in any other factor that may affect demand.

Movement off the Demand Curve

Movement off the demand curve is also called a **change in demand** or shift in demand. Increase or decrease in the demand for a good refers to movement of the quantity demanded off the demand curve. It indicates movement in demand even when the price of a commodity does not change. Thus, change in demand occurs when something (other than the price of the commodity) prompts consumers to buy different amounts at every price.

An increase in demand is denoted by an upward and rightward shift of the demand curve.

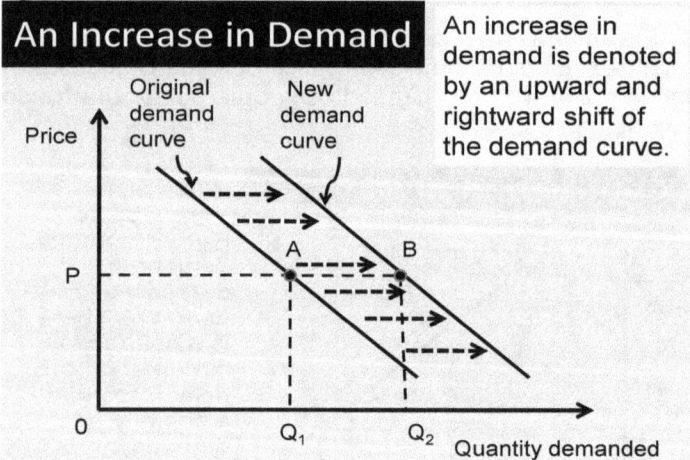

Thus, an **increase in demand** (rise in demand) means that consumers now demand more of a product at each and every price than they did before.

A decrease in demand is denoted by a downward and leftward shift of the demand curve.

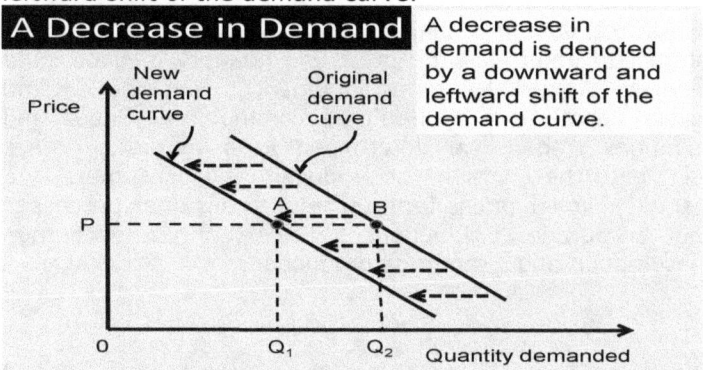

Thus, a **fall in demand** (decrease in demand) means that consumers now demand less of a product at each and every price than they did before.

Factors That Can Cause a Change in Demand

Factors that can cause a change in demand include:
1. A change in income.
2. A change in market size.
3. A change in consumer tastes.
4. A change in consumer expectations.
5. A change in price and availability of substitute goods.
6. A change in price and availability of complementary goods.

Examples on how a change in income may cause a change in demand are the following: An increase in income, *ceteris paribus*, will result into an increase in demand for a normal good. Likewise, a fall in income, *ceteris paribus*, will result into a decrease in demand for a normal good.

5.3   What is a Market?

A **market** is a mechanism by which buyers and sellers interact to determine the price and quantity of goods and services. A market is an arrangement in which buyers and sellers negotiate a well-defined commodity. Prices and quantities traded are determined in a market. Prices coordinate the decisions of producers and consumers in a market. Higher prices tend to reduce consumer purchases and encourage production. Lower prices encourage consumption and discourage production.

5.4   Price Determination by Market Forces

The workings of the market (or price) mechanism are the basis for the market economy system of allocating scarce resources. Price is the signal to the entrepreneur, and price is determined in the market by two opposing forces: supply and demand.
Market price is the term used to describe the price that is arrived at when suppliers and consumers come together. The point of intersection of the two curves (namely demand curve and supply curve) is called the position of market equilibrium.

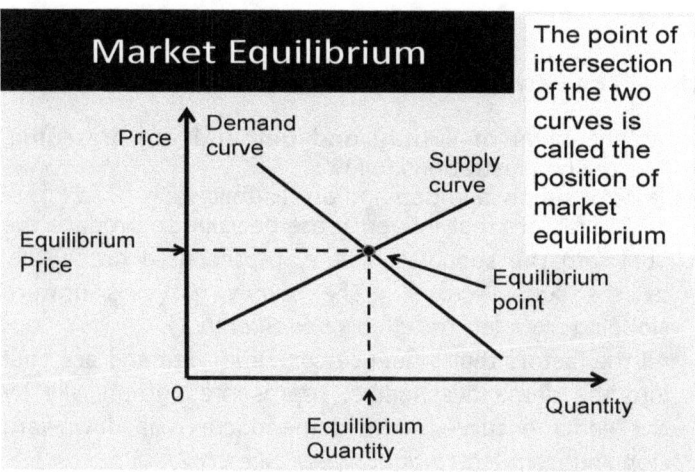

Private entrepreneurs, motivated by maximizing profits, allocate scarce resources to the production of those commodities with rising prices.

The concept of a market in economics is that of a clearing house. Market is the mechanism enabling persons needing a commodity come into direct contact with the persons producing or supplying it. Thus, a market is an institution rather than a place or location. The market as an institution or organization performs a very important role of facilitating exchange between the buyers and sellers of the commodity.

5.5   Characteristics of the Price System

Price works as signals and incentives. In a market economy, the price system has the following characteristics:
1. It is neutral.
2. It is market driven.
3. It is flexible.
4. It is efficient.

5.6   The Laws of Supply and Demand

Firstly, the **laws of supply and demand** are presented, and, secondly, illustrations follow:

The laws of supply and demand are as follows:

1. All the factors that influence the decision to produce are built into the supply schedule, represented graphically by the supply curve.   The supply curve is upward slopping from left to right. *(See Sketch 1).*

2. All the factors that influence consumer demand are built into the demand schedule, represented graphically by the demand curve.   The demand curve is downward slopping from left to right. *(See Sketch 2).*

3. The equilibrium price and the equilibrium quantity traded in the market are achieved at intersection of the supply and demand curves.   It is these two curves together which determine the market price: Price is only partly decided by the cost of production, only partly decided by consumer tastes and incomes. *(See Sketch 3).*

4. An increase in supply shifts the supply curve to the right and lowers the market price, all other factors remaining constant. *(See Sketch 4a).*

5. A reduction in supply shifts the supply curve to the left and increases the market price, all other factors remaining constant. *(See Sketch 4b).*

6. An increase in demand shifts the demand curve to the right and increases the market price, all other factors remaining constant. *(See Sketch 5a).*

7. A reduction in demand shifts the demand curve to the left and reduces the market price, all other factors remaining constant. *(See Sketch 5b).*

Illustrations of the Laws of Supply and Demand

Question: With the aid of sketches explain how supply and demand may determine price.

Suggested answer: The modern supply and demand theory of price can be outlined as shown in *Sketches 1 through 5 below.* Supply and demand are considered, in Marshall's phrase, as "the two blades of a scissors", interacting and determining price in the competitive market. Note that in illustrations in this chapter "Price" stands for the price of the commodity per unit, while "Quantity" is the quantity of the commodity per time period.

Sketch 1:   Supply
From the side of supply, the marginal cost is an indicator to suppliers of the price they will require for a given quantity of the product at a particular time. *Law: The higher the price of a commodity, the greater will be the amount supplied, other things being equal.*

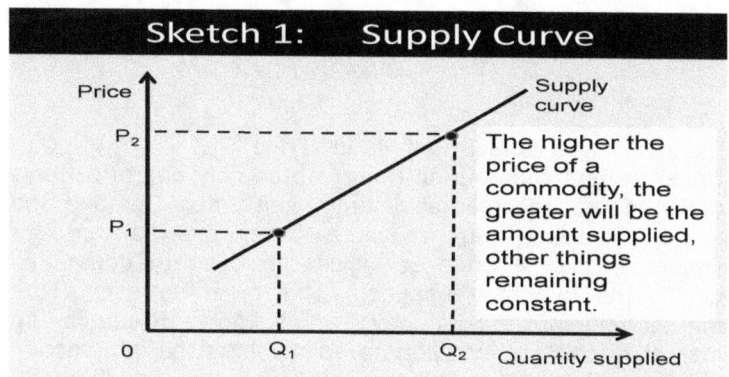

Sketch 2:   Demand
From the side of demand, the marginal utility of a
commodity determines the value placed by consumers on a
given quantity of the commodity at a particular time. *Law:*
        *The lower the price of a commodity, the greater will
be the quantity demanded, other things being equal.*

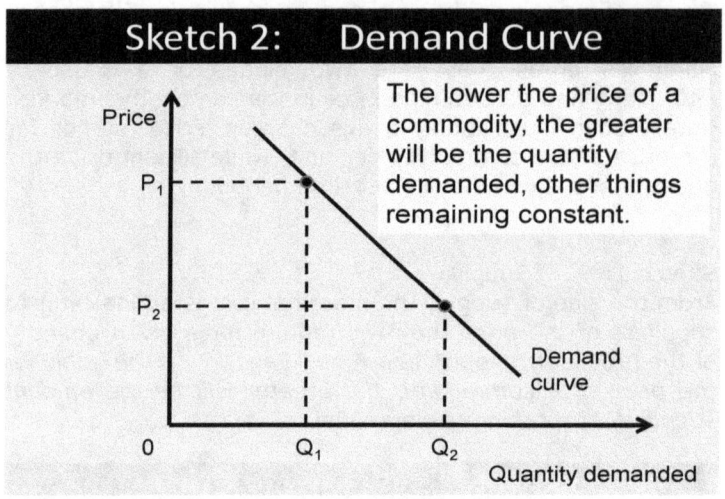

Sketch 3:   Equilibrium Market Price
Under perfect competition there can be only one price for a
commodity in the market at any given time. Demand and
supply fluctuate, but reach a temporary balance (or
equilibrium) at a price at which the quantity demanded
equals the quantity supplied. This price represents the
market value of the commodity, and is known as equilibrium
market price. The equilibrium point marks the intersection
of the supply and demand curves. *Law: Equilibrium
price is established where the quantities demanded and
supplied are equal.*

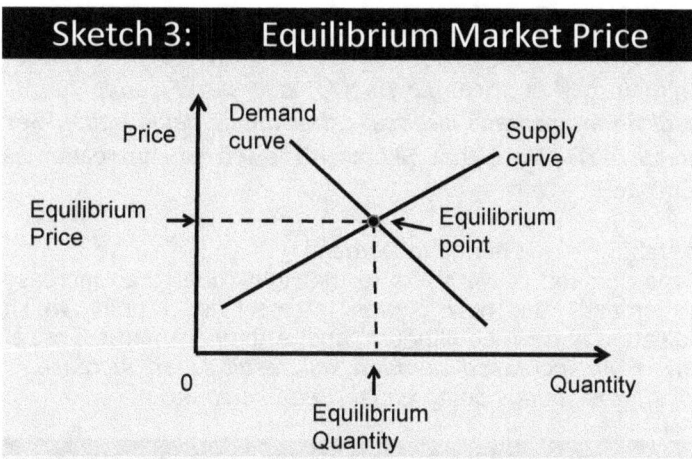

Sketch 3:   Equilibrium Market Price

Equilibrium price is established where the quantities demanded and supplied are equal.

Sketch 4:   Change in Supply
If the supply curve shifts to the right (due to an increase in supply) the new equilibrium point indicates a lower market price. *Law: An increased supply will result in a fall in price, other things being equal.(See Sketch 4a).*

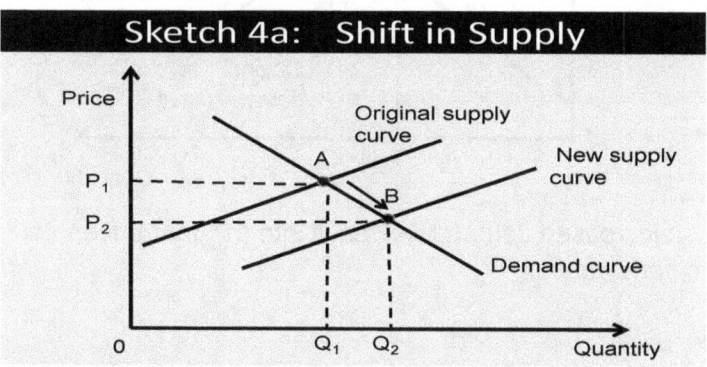

Sketch 4a: Shift in Supply

An increase in supply will result in a fall in price, *ceteris paribus.*

On the other hand, if the supply curve shifts to the left (due to a reduction in supply) the new equilibrium point indicates a higher market price. *Law: A decreased supply will result in an increase in price, other things being equal.(See Sketch 4b).* Note that Sketch 4b is left to the reader as homework.

Sketch 5:   Change in Demand
If the demand curve shifts to the right (due to an increase in demand) the new curves intersect at a point which indicates a new equilibrium and a higher market price. *Law: An increased demand will result in an increase in price, other things being equal (See Sketch 5a).*

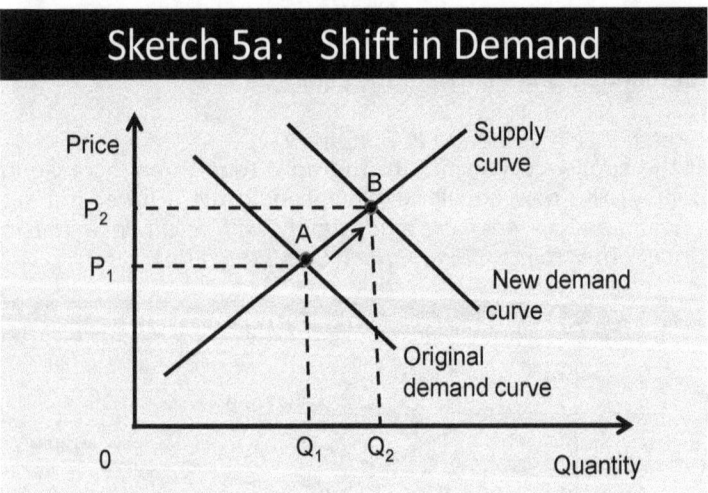

Sketch 5a: Shift in Demand

An increased demand will result into a higher price, *ceteris paribus*.

On the other hand, if the demand curve shifts to the left (due to a reduction in demand) the new curves intersect at a point which indicates a new equilibrium and a lower market price. *Law: A decreased demand will result in an increase in price, other things being equal.(See Sketch 5b).* Note that Sketch 5b is left to the reader as homework. . Also note that "Other things being equal" is commonly written as *ceteris paribus*.

5.7   Shifts in Supply and Demand

The effects of shifts in supply and demand are illustrated in Sketches 4 and 5 above. Shifts in supply are also called movement off the supply curve. Shifts in demand are also called movement off the demand curve.

5.8   The Roles of Price in a Free Market Economy

The **roles of price** in a free market economy are as follows:
1. Price facilitates the determination of what and how each commodity is to be produced.
2. Price facilitates the allocation of resources.
3. Price facilitates the determination of flow of income.
4. Price facilitates the distribution of commodities over time.
5. Price signals reduce government planning burden.

The Prerequisites for the Existence of a Market

Prerequisites for the existence of the market are as follows:
1. Existence of commodities.
2. Existence of buyers and sellers.
3. An area or region.
4. Contact between buyers and sellers.
5. One price for every commodity in a specific period of time.

The Functions of a Market

The functions of a market in a free economy market are as follows:
1. A market facilitates transactions.
2. A market is a source of supply.
3. A market facilitates contact between buyers and sellers.
4. A market facilitates price determination and stabilization.
5. A market increases production.

Price Determination in a Market

In a market, prices may be determined by haggling; fixing by treaties; sales auction; and forces of demand and supply.

Review Questions

1. Distinguish between a change in demand and a change in quantity demanded? Illustrate with diagrams.
2. Define supply and outline what the law of supply says.
3. Define demand and outline what the law of demand says.
4. Explain how supply and demand may determine price in a free market economy.
5. Identify the roles of price in a free market economy.

Chapter Six

Market Structures

Market Structures

Key Terms	Objectives
Market structure, pure competition, monopolistic competition, oligopoly, monopoly *A market structure* is an economic model that helps economists to examine the nature and degree of competition among businesses in the same industry	In this chapter, you will ❏ identify features that help economists to examine the amount of competition in the market ❏ identify factors which determine the structure of the market ❏ understand models of market structure classified mainly according to number of sellers ❏ understand how monopolies can restrict competition

6.1 Reasons for Competition among Firms

Competition involves all the actions that sellers, acting independently, take to get buyers to purchase their products. In a competitive market firms compete with each other. Possible **reasons for competition** among firms include:

1. Efforts to increase customer base.
2. Efforts to increase sales.

3. Efforts to expand market share.
4. Efforts to achieve product superiority.
5. Efforts to enhance image.
6. Efforts to maximize profits.

Features to Examine the Amount of Competition

In economics, **market structure** describes how a market is organized in terms of how much competition there is, usually on the supply side. A market structure is an economic model that helps economists to examine the nature and degree of competition among businesses in the same industry.

The following features enable economists to examine the amount of competition in a market:
1. The amount of control a firm or group of firms has over market price.
2. The amount of influence a firm or group of firms has over market price.
3. The freedom new suppliers have to enter a market.
4. Barriers to entry that restrict new competition.

Competitive Pricing Strategies

Firms can compete with each other through price competition or through non-price competition. Possible **competitive pricing strategies** include:
1. Penetration price.
2. Expansion pricing.
3. Market skimming (price creaming).
4. Price wars.
5. Price leadership.
6. Destruction pricing (predatory pricing).

Determinants of the Extent of the Market

The **extent of the market** means the size of the market. The factors which determine the extent of a market include the following:
1. Extent of demand and supply.
2. Means of transport and communication.
3. Banking and monetary services.
4. Government policy.
5. Peace and security.
1. Grading.
2. Packaging.
3. Sanitary condition of the market place.
4. Location of the market.

Industry and Market

Industry is a group of firms producing the same product or similar products, for example the textile or paper industry. Industry may also mean a group of firms using the same process or raw material, for example the chemical industry or the electronic industry. Thus an industry is defined in terms of supply or production.

On the other hand, a market is a group of firms supplying products that buyers consider to be substitutes. Thus, a market is defined from the point of view of buyers or demand.

The terms 'industry' and 'market' do not always mean the same thing. For instance, the footwear market consists of products that are supplied by more than one industry, namely, leather, rubber, and plastic. The aluminium industry caters to markets for several products like utensils, packaging material, building material, etc.

Meaning of Structure of the Market

The conduct of the market structure means the manner and the extent to which firms constituting a particular market are related to each other. Since firms operating in the same market are related to each other as competitors or rivals, the term **structure of the market** refers to the degree of competition prevailing in that market.

Factors Which Determine the Structure of a Market

The factors which determine the structure of a market are called structural variables. These factors include:

1) number of independent sellers and buyers
   a) large
   b) few
   c) two
   d) one
2) degree of seller-concentration
   a) non-existence
   b) low
   c) medium
   d) high
3) product differentiation
   a) perfect substitutes or homogeneous products
   b) close substitutes or slight differentiation in form of different brands
   c) remote substitutes
   d) no substitutes

4) condition of entry
   a) free or easy entry
   b) difficult entry
   c) entry barred or impossible

Classification of Markets

Classification of markets may be either through market types or through market structures. Such a classification is as follows:
1) Market types
   a) Commodity market
   b) Factor market
      i) Labour market
      ii) Capital market
      iii) Land market
   c) Financial market or money market
      i) Foreign exchange market
      ii) Security market
2) Market structures
   a) Perfect competition
   b) Imperfect competition
      i) Monopolistic competition
      ii) Oligopoly
      iii) duopoly
   c) Monopoly

6.2 Models of Market Structures

Models of market structure, classified mainly according to number of sellers, are as follows
1. Pure competition.
2. Monopolistic competition.
3. Oligopoly.
4. Monopoly.

Sometimes the models of market structure are seen as a spectrum. Generally a spectrum of markets, classified according to the number of producers, starts from a very large number of suppliers to a single supplier

Pure Competition

Pure (Perfect) competition is characterized as follows:
1. Large number of independent sellers.
2. Seller concentration is non-existent (i.e., all firms have insignificant and nearly equal market share).
3. Product differentiation is non-existent. There are homogeneous products.
4. Free or easy condition of entry.

Monopolistic Competition

Monopolistic competition is characterized as follows:
1. Large number of independent firms.
2. Non-existent or low seller concentration.
3. Slight product differentiation. Products are close substitutes.
4. Free or easy condition of entry.

Oligopoly

Oligopoly is characterized as follows:
1. Few numbers of independent firms.
2. Medium or high seller concentration.
3. Non-existent or slight product differentiation. Products may be homogeneous or close substitutes.
4. Difficult condition of entry. Hence the number of firms remains small and concentration continues to be medium or high even in the long run.

Duopoly

Duopoly is a special case of oligopoly. Duopoly is characterized as follows:
1. Two independent firms.
2. Non-existent or slight product differentiation. Products may be homogeneous or close substitutes.
3. High seller concentration.
4. Very difficult or impossible condition of entry. Hence two sellers continue to control the market even in the long run.

Pure Monopoly

Monopoly is characterized as follows:
1. One seller.
2. Very high seller concentration. One seller controlling almost 100 percent of total supply.
3. Products of related industries are remote substitutes.
4. Barred or impossible condition of entry. In the case of public utilities there is a legal bar. Hence the market remains in the control of one firm even in the long run.

6.3   Monopolies Can Restrict Competition

Monopolies can restrict competition. There are natural barriers to entry and artificial barriers to entry.

Possible Natural Barriers to Entry

Natural barriers to entry include:
1. Economies of scale.
2. Capital size.
3. Historical reasons.
4. Legal consideration

Possible Artificial Barriers to Entry

Artificial barriers to entry include:
1. Restrictions on supplies.
2. Predatory pricing.
3. Exclusive dealings.
4. Full line forcing.

Types of Monopolies

Types of monopolies are:
1. Natural monopolies.
2. Government monopolies.
3. Technological monopolies.
4. Geographic monopoly.

Disadvantages of Monopolies

Disadvantages of monopoly may include:
1. Less consumer choice.
2. Higher prices.
3. Lower product quality.
4. X inefficiency.
5. The need for regulation.

Possible Advantages of Monopolies

Some advantages of monopolies are:
1. Efficiency in providing public utilities.
2. Avoidance of reduplication of efforts in producing a standardized commodity.

Review Questions

1. Identify features that help economists to examine the amount of competition in the market.
2. Identify factors which determine the structure of the market.
3. Mention the models of market structure classified mainly according to number of sellers.
4. How do monopolies restrict competition?

Chapter Seven
Distribution

Distribution

Key Terms	Objectives
Distribution, labour market, wages, interest income, rental income, income from profit, income inequalities	In this chapter, you will
	❑ name rewards given to various factors of production
	❑ identify possible reasons for wage differentials
Each factor of production earns a *reward* due to its contribution in production	❑ recognize why people in the same job earn different amounts
	❑ note the possibility for government interference in labour market
	❑ understand causes of income inequalities

7.1   Rewards to Factors of production

Factors of production receive rewards for their contribution in the production process.
Wages income is a reward to labour.
Interest income is a reward to capital.
Rental income is a reward to land.

Entrepreneurs receive **income from profit**. Sole proprietors receive profit. Also shareholders, who may not be involved directly in the management of firms, receive income from profit. Profit is a reward to entrepreneurs.

7.2   Wages

The price of labour is determined in the labour market. The forces of demand for labour and supply of labour determine the price of labour. The price of labour is called wages.

- If there is a rightward shift in the demand for labour, other factors remaining constant, then wages rises.
- If there is a rightward shift in the supply of labour, other factors remaining constant, then wages falls.

Why Do People Earn Different Amounts?

If labour markets were perfect, then people doing the same activity under similar circumstances would earn equal amounts of wages. But labour markets are characterized by imperfections. Possible reasons for **wage differentials** include:
1. Different abilities and qualifications.
2. 'Dirty' jobs and unsociable hours.
3. Satisfaction.
4. Lack of information about jobs and wages.
5. Immobility.
6. Fringe benefits.

Why Do People in the Same Job Earn Different Amounts?

People in the same job may earn different amounts due to:
1. Regional differences in labour market condition.
2. Length of service.
3. Local pay agreements.
4. Non-wage rewards.
5. Discrimination.

7.3 Government Intervention in Labour Markets

Government may interfere in labour market. Possible reasons are:
1. To pay for its employees. Government may be a major employer of teachers, doctors, civil servants, army personnel, and other public sector workers.
2. To protect the rights of employees and employers.
3. To outlaw and regulate the restrictive practices of powerful trade unions and employers.
4. To raise the wages of very low-paid workers.
5. To reduce unemployment.
6. To stop discrimination.

7.4 Income Inequality

Income inequalities exist in society. It is the objective of government to try to reduce the inequalities.

The causes of **income inequalities** may include:
1. Natural ability.
2. Education, training, and opportunity.
3. Property ownership.
4. Ability to influence wages and salaries.
5. Luck.
6. Weeks worked.
7. Age.

All modern governments try, in one way or another, to intervene in the economy so as to provide for re-distribution of income wherever the status quo is viewed as inappropriate.

Review Questions

1. Name rewards given to various factors of production.
2. Identify possible reasons for wage differentials.
3. Why people in the same job earn different amounts?
4. Why do governments interfere in labour markets?
5. Mention possible causes of income inequalities.

Chapter Eight

Consumption and Savings

Consumption and Savings

Key Terms	Objectives
Consumption, savings, borrowing, financial intermediaries, investment *Financial intermediaries* have a special role to channel savings into investment	In this chapter, you will ❑ identify determinants of consumption ❑ describe possible reasons for saving ❑ identify the determinants of the level of borrowing among consumers ❑ identify the factors affecting saving ❑ note the role of financial intermediaries in channeling savings into investment

8.1   Consumption

Determinants of **consumption**, that is, factors influencing consumer choice, include:
1. The size of income.
2. The distribution of income.
3. Cost of credit.
4. Availability of credit.
5. Government policy.

8.2   Savings

What determine savings?   **Saving** involves a person delaying consumption until some later time when they withdraw and spend their savings plus any interest. Possible reasons for saving are:
1. For consumption.
2. For interest rates.
3. For consumer confidence.
4. For availability of saving schemes.

8.3   Borrowing

Why do people borrow money?   Consumers may **borrow** money to increase their expenditure on goods and services. Possible determinants of the level of borrowing include:
1. Interest rates.
2. Wealth.
3. Consumer confidence.
4. Ways of borrowing and the availability of credit.

8.4   Factors Affecting Savings

Factors affecting savings, that is, the determinants of savings include:
1. The size of income.
2. The distribution of income.
3. Interest rates.
4. Availability of financial institutions.
5. Government policy.

8.5   Savings and Investment

Determinants of **investment** include:
1. Expected yield from investment.
2. The cost of investment.
3. New techniques and inventions.
4. Government policy.

8.6   Financial Intermediaries

Financial intermediaries help the economy to channel funds from economic agents with surplus funds to economic agents with deficit funds. Hence, the financial institutions facilitate savings and investments.

Review Questions

1. Identify the determinants of consumption.
2. Describe the possible reasons for saving.
3. Identify the determinants of the level of borrowing among consumers.
4. Identify the factors affecting saving.
5. Describe how the financial intermediaries are channeling savings into investment.

Chapter Nine

Government Expenditures and Revenues

Government Expenditures and Revenues

Key Terms

Government expenditures, government revenues, distributive motive, efficiency motive, public goods, private sector, public sector, macroeconomic policy objectives and tools

Government intervention in the economy is through the ways in which it gets its revenues and through the ways in which it spends it.

Objectives

In this chapter, you will
❏ understand why government intervene in the economy
❏ identify categories of government expenditures
❏ identify sources of government revenues
❏ identify functions of taxation and understand features of a good tax system

9.1   Government Intervention in the Economy

Governments manage the economy to achieve their objectives. They can do this by the following ways:
1.   Controlling the amount of money in the economy.
2.   Changing how they raise and spend money.
3.   Controlling how people behave by law.

The **public sector** is the portion of the economy that provides certain goods and services that the market system might fail to provide and redistribute income among groups by means of taxation.

Government intervention in the economy is through the ways in which it gets its revenues and through the ways in which it spends it. The power of the public sector arises from its ability to collect taxes and spend them.

The primary purpose of taxation is to move resources out of the private sector and into the public sector. But economists have long recognized that taxation also has significant secondary effects on the way resources are allocated within the private sector. Objectives of government expenditure include a distributive motive (distributing wealth from one group to another) and an efficiency motive (the transfer of resources from less productive uses in the private sector to more valuable uses in the public sector).

The three broad elements of public finance are:
1. Expenditure.
2. Income.
3. Borrowing.

There are three main economic functions of governments in a market economy. Those functions are:
1. Increasing efficiency.
2. Promoting equity.
3. Fostering macroeconomic stability.

Arguments for Government Intervention in the Economy

The state may choose to **intervene in the economy** for the following reasons:
1. To provide public goods.

2. To transfer or re-distribute wealth between members of society.
3. To pursue macroeconomic policy objectives, notably economic growth, full employment, price stability and balance of payment equilibrium.
4. To achieve greater economic efficiency.
5. To influence what is consumed and what is produced within the economy.

The basic justification for government intervention in the economy are that the free market, left on its own, might not work, or that it might work but in an undesirable way. Thus, governments have three main economic functions in a market economy. These functions are: increasing **efficiency** (by promoting competition, curbing externalities like pollution, and providing public goods); promoting **equity** (by using tax and expenditure programs to redistribute income toward particular groups); and fostering **macroeconomic stability and growth** (that is, reducing unemployment and inflation while encouraging growth through fiscal policy and monetary regulation). The ultimate objectives of monetary and fiscal policies are to encourage rapid growth (i.e., a high and growing level of national output), low unemployment, and stable prices.

Objections to Government Intervention

Objections to government intervention in the economy, which are arguments against government intervention in the economy, include the following:
1. Government will allocate production resources inefficiently and will tend to use resources inefficiently.

2. A 'free-market economy' will use resources more effectively and efficiently, and so create faster economic growth which will benefit a society as a whole.
3. In its attempts to control the economy, a government may actually do more harm than good.
4. Governments are bureaucratic and will respond only very slowly to changes in market conditions.
5. In order to give private enterprise freedom to develop the economy, the government should reduce the amount and scope of its regulations.

9.2   Government Expenditures

Government expenditures are usually directed to the following functions:
1. Health and welfare.
2. Economic development and support.
3. Public debt.
4. Defense.
5. Fiscal transfers to regions and local authorities.
6. Transport and communications.
7. All other functions such as general government services, education assistance, internal overhead expenses, foreign affairs, culture and recreation.

Reasons for Government Expenditure

Reasons for government expenditures include the arguments in favour of government intervention in the economy, and specially to provide for the functions to which government expenditures are directed to.

Growth in Government Spending

Generally there is a tendency for citizens to demand more from their governments. The economic principle is generally as follows: if citizens demand more government spending, then they must prepare themselves for an increase in taxation if other factors remain constant. Otherwise the government should in a short run rely on borrowing. The long run effects of borrowing, if not done wisely, are an increased burden to the society.

9.3   Government Revenues

In order to spend the government should have revenues. The size of the revenues will somehow affect the ability of the government to spend.

Sources of Government Revenues

Possible **sources of Government revenues** include:
1. Taxes.
2. Grants.
3. Fees.
4. Fines.
5. Profits of public enterprises.

Progressive, Proportional, and Regressive Taxation

All the taxes in a country are together called the **tax system**. Three possible tax systems are:
1. Progressive.
2. Regressive.
3. Proportional

A progressive tax system is one where the proportion of income taken in taxation rises as income rise. A regressive tax system takes a smaller proportion of income in tax as income rises. A proportional tax is one where the proportion of income taken in tax is the same whatever the level of income. Governments must decide whether they want a progressive, regressive, or a proportional tax system.

Direct and Indirect Tax

The two main **types of taxes** are direct taxes and indirect taxes. Direct taxes are taken directly from a person or firm from their incomes or wealth. Indirect taxes are taxes taken only indirectly from incomes when they are spent on goods and services, and they are normally collected from those people or firms selling those goods and services.

The following are the advantages of indirect taxes:
1. Revenue is obtained.
2. Redistribution is achieved.
3. Ability to pay is considered.

The following are the disadvantages of direct tax:
1. Work incentive is reduced.
2. Enterprise is discouraged.
3. Tax evasion is encouraged.

Types of indirect taxes include:
1. Value added tax (VAT).
2. Tariffs.
3. Excise duties.
4. User taxes or charges.

The following are the advantages of indirect taxes:
1. Cost of collection is minimal.
2. Wider tax base is possible.
3. Selective aims are possible.

The following are the disadvantages of indirect taxes:
1. Uncertainty.
2. Regressive.
3. Inflation.

Functions of Taxation

The **functions of taxation** are as follows:
1. To raise revenue for the government.
2. To discourage certain activities regarded as undesirable.
3. To cause certain products to be priced while taking into account their social costs.
4. To redistribute wealth.
5. To protect domestic industries from foreign competition.
6. To provide a stabilizing effect on national income.

Features of a Good Tax System

The features of a good tax system, also called the **canons of taxation**, are as follows:
1. Taxes should be fair or 'equitable'.
2. The tax should be 'certain' and easily understood by all concerned.
3. The payment of tax should ideally be related to how and when people receive and spend their income and should therefore be convenient to pay.
4. The cost of collection should be small relative to yield.
5. Taxes should be adjustable.
6. Taxes should not harm initiative.
7. Evasion must be difficult.

9.4 Economic Policy Tools

A government may use a number of different **policy tools** in order to try to achieve its objectives. These tools are as follows:
1. Monetary policy.
2. Fiscal policy.
3. Prices and incomes policy.
4. Exchange rate policy.
5. Import controls.

A government might adopt a policy mix of monetary policy, fiscal policy and exchange rate policy in its attempts to achieve its economic objectives.

Here we distinguish between monetary and fiscal policy. **Monetary policies** are policies implemented by monetary authorities (i.e., the Treasury and the Central Bank) and are aimed at influencing the quantity of money, the price of money (interest rates) and the availability of credit in the economy.

Fiscal policy is concerned with action by the government to spend money, or to collect money in taxes, with the purpose of influencing the condition of the national economy.

A government might intervene in the economy by:

1. Spending more money without collecting more in taxes; or
2. Collecting more in taxes without increasing spending; or
3. Collecting more in taxes in order to increase spending, thus diverting income from one part of the economy to another

A budget surplus occurs when the government takes in more than it spends in a particular year. A budget deficit occurs when government spends more than it takes in. Deficit spending is a government practice of spending more than it takes for a specific budget year. Deficit spending results into national debt. The national debt is the money that the government owes.

Causes of deficit spending may include the following:

1. National emergencies.
2. Need for public goods and services.
3. Stabilization of the economy.
4. Role of government in society.

Review Questions

1. Provide arguments for government intervention in the economy.
2. Provide arguments against government intervention in the economy.
3. Identify categories of government expenditures.
4. Identify sources of government revenues.
5. Identify functions of taxation.
6. Mention the features of a good tax system.

Chapter Ten

Money and Banking

Money and Banking

Key Terms	Objectives
Money, means of exchange, unit of account, standard of deferred payment, store of value, qualities of money, barter, banking system, credit creation, central bank, monetary policy *Money* is a commodity that everyone is willing to accept in exchange for all goods and services in a particular society in a given period of time	In this chapter, you will ❏ define and describe the functions of money ❏ identify qualities of money ❏ understand the importance of money in an economy ❏ understand the process of credit creation through the banking system ❏ note the role of the central bank as the hub of the banking system

10.1 Money

"What is money?" "Why is money important in the economy of a modern society?" Attempts to define money have traditionally started with identifying the following issues:

1. What are the functions of money?
2. What particular characteristics should money have in order that it can perform its functions efficiently and effectively?

Our primitive ancestors relied on direct swapping of goods and services they produced. That early form of exchange is known as barter.

During the **barter trade** goods were exchanged with other goods wherever there was a double coincidence of wants. There were some inconveniences of the barter system of trade. Bartering is a most inconvenient way to carry out a business.

Problems of bartering include:

1. Fixing a rate of exchange.
2. Finding someone to swap with.
3. Trying to save.

The introduction of money helped to solve the inconveniences of bartering. **Money** is a commodity that everyone is willing to accept in exchange for all goods and services in a particular society in a given period of time. Money overcomes a problem of needing a double coincidence of wants.

Functions of Money (Uses of Money)

We need money because it has qualities which enable it to do its functions. The **functions of money** are:

1. Money as a means of exchange.
2. Money as a unit of account.
3. Money as a standard of deferred payment.
4. Money as a store of value.

Money is a **means of exchange** (i.e., a medium of exchange). This is the most important function of money in an economy, because without money, the only way of exchanging goods and services would be by means of barter. The barter economy has enormous limitations.

A monetary economy is the only alternative to a barter economy, and is a means of encouraging economic development and growth. Money provides a flexible, precise, and convenient way to exchange goods and services.

Money is a **unit of account** (i.e., a measure of value). Money provides a way to express and measure the relative costs of goods and services. Money provides a way to compare the worthy of different goods and services.

Money is a **standard of deferred payment**. How can somebody buy goods and services on credit? Money as a standard of deferred payment performs that function.

Money is a **store of value**. A store of value is something that holds its value over time. Money can be saved for later use because it can be exchanged at any time for goods and services.

Attributes of Money (Qualities of Money)

The qualities or characteristics or **attributes of money** are as follows:
1. Acceptability.
2. Divisibility.
3. Durability.
4. Some degree of scarcity.
5. Uniformity or 'homogeneity'.
6. Portability.
7. Some stability of value.

Importance of Money in an Economy

Money is important because it encourages specialization. If people specialize they must trade. But in a barter system trade is difficult. Money overcomes a problem of needing a double coincidence of wants. Money encourages specialization by making trade easier and so enables an economy to increase the level of national income and allow people to enjoy a much higher standard living.

Money is needed by consumers, firms, and government to make payments to buy resources, and goods and services. The banking system can provide this money and make it easier to make payments. Therefore, as the output of an economy grows and more trade takes place, so the banking system must develop and create more money.

Types of Money

There are three types of money namely commodity money, representative money, and fiat money. Commodity money has intrinsic value based on the material from which it is made. Representative money is backed by something tangible. Fiat money is declared by government and accepted by citizens to have worth.

Money in Tanzania

What serves as money in Tanzania includes currency (that is, paper money and coins), and demand deposits. Economists use various instruments to measure the supply of money in an economy.

Money in the narrowest sense is that which can be immediately used for transactions. Economists call it M1. M1 consists of currency, demand deposits, and other checkable deposits. M2 is a broader measure of money supply. It consists of M1 plus various kinds of near money (for instance saving deposits) as defined by the monetary authorities from time to time.

10.2   Banking System

The **banking system** consists of the commercial banks, other banking institutions, and the central bank. Banks are financial institutions in the money market.   Banks are financial intermediaries between customers who want to deposit money and customers who want to borrow money.

Roles of Banks in the Economy

Banks have many roles including participation in the process of credit creation.

The functions of **commercial banks** are as follows:

1. Commercial banks are providing a payment mechanism, which is a way in which individuals, firms and government organizations can make payments to each other.   The banks are also a source from which individuals and firms can obtain notes and coins.

2. Commercial banks are providing a place for individuals, firms and government organizations to store their wealth, for example in current accounts or deposit accounts.   Banks compete with other financial institutions to attract the funds of individuals and firms.

3. Commercial banks are lending money in the form of loans, overdrafts or other specialized schemes.

4. Commercial banks are providing a wide range of services to customers, some of which are not strictly banking activities.

Roles (Functions) of the Central Bank in the Economy

Functions of a **central bank** in an economy are as follows:
1. It has sole right to issue notes and coins.
2. It is the government's bank.
3. It manages the nation's gold and foreign currency reserves.
4. It manages the national debt.
5. It is 'lender of last resort'.
6. It sets the official interest rate.
7. It conducts bank supervision.
8. It participates in the implementation of monetary policy.

An institution which takes the roles of a central bank in Tanzania is called the **Bank of Tanzania** BOT). Monetary policies are policies implemented by the treasury and the Bank of Tanzania (referred jointly as the monetary authorities) and are aimed at influencing the quantity of money, the price of money (interest rates) and the availability of credit in the economy. The central bank is the hub of the banking system.

10.3 The Creation of Money in the Banking System

The **creation of money** in the banking system is also called the process of credit creation. The government can create money simply by printing more. Banks also have the ability to create money! This ability is something that sets banks apart from other financial institutions.

Let us have a look at how the process of credit creation works. If we assume that:
1. There is only one bank in our banking system even though it may have several branches.
2. There is never any shortage of suitable borrowers.
3. Banks only have two assets namely cash and loans, and one liability, namely deposits.
4. Banks need only keep 20% of deposits in cash in order to satisfy customer's demands for cash.

Then we can see the effect of bank lending on the level of bank deposits.
As our starting point let us say that someone deposits TZS 10000 in a new account at the bank. (Here, TZS is an abbreviation for the Tanzanian currency, i. e., Tshs = Tanzanian shillings). An extract from the balance sheet at the bank would look like this:

Assets		Liabilities	
	Tshs		Tshs
Cash	1000	Deposits	10000

Now the banks only needs to keep 20% of this deposit in cash and can therefore lend 80%. Distributing the assets in this way gives us:

Assets			Liabilities		
		Tshs			Tshs
Cash		2000	Deposits		10000
Loans		8000			
		10000			10000

But why do people borrow money? People borrow money in order to spend it!

In a system with one bank and no cash leaks, when the person who borrowed Tshs 8000 buys say, a radio, the radio dealer will certainly put this money back into the bank at the end of the day. The bank will see this Tshs 8000 as a new deposit and the balance sheet extract will look like this:

Assets		Liabilities	
	Tshs		Tshs
Cash	10000	Deposits	18000
Loans	8000		
	_18000_		_18000_

If the bank only needs 20% of deposits in cash then it is holding too much and should lend another 6400 to restore the balance:

Assets		Liabilities	
	Tshs		Tshs
Cash	3600	Deposits	18000
Loans	14400		
	_18000_		_18000_

The person who borrowed 6400 will spend it and, as there are no leaks, it will find its way back to the bank. The bank will see this as a new deposit and the balance sheet will look like this:

Assets			Liabilities	
	Tshs			Tshs
Cash	10000		Deposits	2400
Loans	14400			
	24400			24400

Too much cash once again and so we can lend some more. We only need to keep 4880 in cash so we can lend an additional 5120:

Assets			Liabilities	
	Tshs			Tshs
Cash	4880		Deposits	24400
Loans	19520			
	24400			24400

This will find its way to the bank as a new deposit:

Assets			Liabilities		
	Tshs			Tshs	
Cash	10000		Deposits	29520	
Loans	19520				
	29520			29520	

And so the process goes on until many balance sheets later ...

Assets			Liabilities		
	Tshs			Tshs	
Cash	10000		Deposits	50000	
Loans	40000				
	50000			50000	

The Credit Multiplier

How do we know that this will be the result? We have a progression which can be solved arithmetically.   The deposits will be raised by the reciprocal of the cash ratio we were using.   The ratio was 20% or 1/5 and therefore the deposits will increase five fold before the process comes to an end.   We would say that we have a credit multiplier of five. If we define money as bank deposits and cash then the banking system in our example has turned a money supply of Tshs 10000 into a money supply of Tshs 50000. Where did the other Tshs 40000 come from? The bank has created it. It doesn't really exist except as entries on the accounts of the depositors.

Review Questions

1. Define and describe the functions of money.
2. Identify qualities of money.
3. Money is important in an economy. Justify.
4. Mention the functions of commercial banks.
5. Mention the functions of the Bank of Tanzania.
6. Justify the following statement: "The central bank is the hub of the banking system".
7. Describe the process of credit creation through the banking system.

Chapter Eleven

Economic Performance

Economic Performance

Key Terms	Objectives
National income, 'national' versus 'domestic', 'gross' versus 'net', 'at factor cost' versus 'at market prices', GDP, NNP, exports, imports, capital consumption, taxes, subsidies, net property income from abroad	In this chapter, you will
	❏ identify the macroeconomic aggregates
	❏ define national income
	❏ identify the three methods of measuring the national income
The national income is the money value all goods and services produced in an economy over a given period of time	❏ mention the uses of national income statistics
	❏ identify the determinants of national income

11.1   Macroeconomic Aggregates

Macroeconomic aggregates are used to evaluate the performance of an economy. Some of these are:
1. The aggregate output level.
2. The aggregate price level.

3. The aggregate consumption level.
4. The aggregate investment level.
5. The balance of payments.

Economists have recognized that the determinants of national income are changes in aggregate consumption levels, changes in aggregate investment levels, and balance of payments. Obviously, changes in national income may be the result of some combination of the above factors. All economic agents have their roles in the performance of an economy, but ultimately the government has to play a crucial role because there are policy tools that are at the disposal of the government. For instance, Government has the power to influence (if only in the short run) by using: fiscal policy, that is, changes in taxes and government spending; and monetary policy, that is, changes in the supply of money and interest rates.
Usually the economic performance of a nation is gauged by the aggregate output. That is why a great deal of effort is made so as to measure it accurately and to keep a record of all determinants that may affect the aggregate output.

11.2   Meaning of National Income

The **national income** is the money value of all goods and services produced in an economy over a given period of time. Precisely, the national income is the **net national product at factor cost**. The national income is an aggregate output which is seen as an indicator of the level of economic activity.

11.3   The Circular Flow of Income

Economists provide a model to help us conceptualize how economic activity takes place in a system and how this level of economic activity can be quantified. The model is the fundamental **circular flow model**.

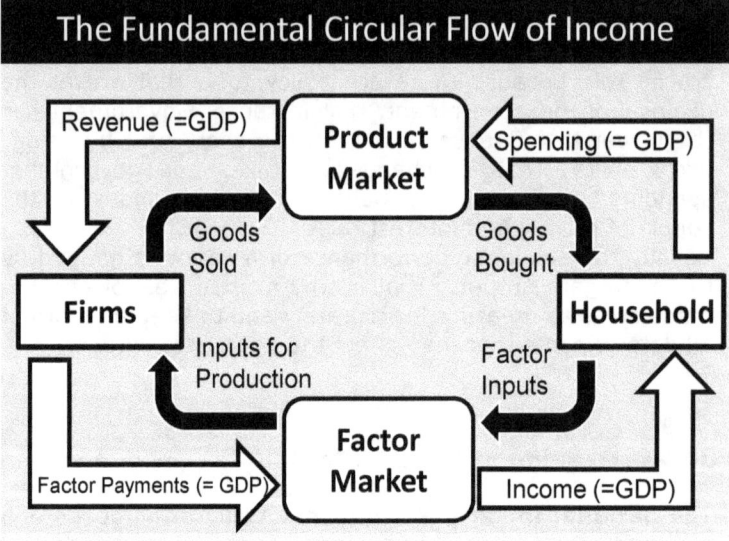

The Fundamental Circular Flow of Income

Aggregate Output = Factor Income = Expenditure

The circular flow model is a tool for understanding the relationships among economic decision makers and various markets.

11.4   Measuring the National Income

The Measurement of National Income is done through various ways. The aggregate output is the value of all final goods and services produced in a country during a period of time.   Under circular flow model, aggregate output = aggregate income = aggregate expenditure.

How national income is measured? There are three methods of measuring (calculating) national income.

Measurement of national income is through:
1. The output method.
2. The expenditure method.
3. The income method.

All methods lead to the same result because they measure the same thing.

The Output Method

The **output method** adds together the value of all goods and services produced in a country in a year.

Table 1: Output Method of Calculating National Income

		Total Domestic Product	
	Less	Stock appreciation	
	Add	Residual error	
	Equals	Gross Domestic Product at	
	Add	Net property income from abroad	
	Equals	Gross National Product at	
	Less	Capital consumption (depreciatio	
	Equals	National income	

The Expenditure Method

The **expenditure method** adds together all money spent by private citizens, firms and the government within the year.

Table 2: Expenditure Method of Calculating National Income

	Total Domestic Expenditure	
Add	Exports	
Less	Imports	
Equals	Gross Domestic Product at market prices	
Less	Taxes	
Add	Subsidies	
Equals	Gross Domestic Product at factor cost	
Add	Net property income from abroad	
Equals	Gross National Product at factor cost	
Less	Capital consumption (depreciation)	
Equals	National income	

The Income Method

The **income method** adds together all the incomes earned by a country's citizens in a year.

Table 3: Income Method of Calculating National Income

		Total Domestic Income	
	Less	Stock appreciation	
	Plus	Residual error	
	Equals	Gross Domestic Product at factor cost	
	Add	Net property income from abroad	
	Equals	Gross National Product at factor cost	
	Less	Capital consumption (depreciation)	
	Equals	National income	

Terms Used in National Income Accounting

To understand the three methods of measuring national income the meaning of these terms is required:

1. **Stock appreciation**: the value of stocks may have risen due to inflation, and this has no connection with output. This stock appreciation must be excluded from the statistics.
2. **Residual error**: an allowance error made in the calculations. Residual error ensures that equality exists between the three methods.
3. **Net property income from abroad**: this is the net amount of flows of interest, profits and dividends flowing to Tanzanian citizens from abroad and to foreigners from the United Republic of Tanzania (URT). A plus item represents a net inflow into the URT.
4. **Capital consumption** (depreciation): some of the country's output is needed to replace buildings, plant, equipment and vehicles which have become worn out.
5. **Gross Domestic Product** (GDP): the total value of goods and services produced in one country.
6. **GDP at factor cost**: GDP less taxes plus subsidies. GDP at factor cost is what the producer actually receives.
7. **Gross National Product** (GNP): GDP plus net property income from abroad.
8. **GNP at factor cost**: GDP at factor cost plus net property income from abroad.

Difficulties in Measuring the National Income

Difficulties in measuring national income include:
1. Incomplete information.
2. Imputed values.
3. Transfer payments.
4. Double counting.

5. The services of housewives.
6. Inflation.
7. Depreciation.

11.5 The Uses of National Income Statistics

The following are some of the **uses of national income statistics**:
1. National income as an instrument of economic planning and review. This will assist central government in its economic planning.
2. National income as a means of indicating changes in a country's standard of living. This is done to measure the improvement (or deterioration as the case may be) in national wealth and standard of living.
3. National income as a means of comparing the economic performance of different countries. For instance, to compare the wealth of different countries.
4. National income as a measure of the total wealth (standard of living) of a country. National income is commonly measured in terms of national income per head of population.
5. National income as an indicator of changes in the economic growth of a country.

Specifically, using the output method it is possible:
• To identify the distribution of industrial activity.
• To identify an industry which is either expanding or is contracting.

Specifically, using the expenditure method it is possible:
• To identify changes in the pattern of consumer spending.
• To identify the levels of imports and the effects of taxes and subsidies.

Specifically, using the incomes method it is possible:
- To identify changes in the distribution of income as between wages (or salaries), rent and incomes from property.
- To show the growth of national income.

Comparisons with Other Countries

It is difficult to compare the national income of one country with that of another for the following reasons:
1. Income and output may be measured in different currencies.
2. Differences in social and political structure are difficult to reconcile.
3. Financial institutions may be at different stages of development.
4. Prices and output may be affected by different systems of taxation and subsidies.

Growth in National Income

There are a number of reasons why governments like to see national income grow:
1. If total output is increasing, then there is a likely chance of more goods and services for everybody.
2. High level of output usually means high levels of employment.
3. If national income is higher, the government itself should be able to raise more funds (for example in taxes) to distribute among the things it is responsible for. This should lead to better roads, housing, health care, defense, and education.

4. Growth in national income might mean that we are making better use of our national resources.

11.6   Determinants of National Income

The **determinants of national income** are the factors which may cause a change in national income. The identity for the expenditure method of the national income provides a starting point to identify the determinants of national income.

$$C + I + G + (X - M) = national \quad income$$

Where C is consumption expenditure, I is investment spending, G is government spending, X are exports, and, M are imports).

Thus, a change in national income can come about from:

1. A change in consumer expenditure.
2. A change in investment spending.
3. A change in government spending.
4. A change in the difference between exports and imports.

The determinants of national income are changes in aggregate consumption levels, aggregate investment levels, and balance of payments. Obviously, changes in national income may be the result of some combination of the above factors.

11.7   A Government Can Influence National Income

A government can influence national income through budgetary policy, monetary policy, incomes policy and external policy.

Budgetary policy is specific measures designed to alter the level of government spending and taxation revenue. Budgetary policy is also referred to as fiscal policy. Budgetary policy aims to alter the level of aggregate demand. Budget is an annual estimate of the revenue to be collected and the expenditure to be made by the government in the subsequent year.

Monetary policy relates to conditions governing the lending and borrowing money in the economy. The Bank of Tanzania implements such policy matters. The components of monetary policy include open market operations, liquidity ratios, control over some interest rates, and influences over non-bank financial intermediaries.

Incomes policy is government policy directed towards the control of all incomes, including profits and wages and salaries.

External policy includes policy related to instruments such as exchange rates, tariffs, and trade agreements.

Review Questions

1. What is the national income?
2. Identify the three methods of measuring the national income.
3. Clearly distinguish GNP at factor cost from GDP at factor cost.
4. Identify the determinants of national income.
5. Mention the uses of national income statistics.
6. Identify ways through which a government can influence the national income.
7. "Usually the economic performance of a nation is gauged by the aggregate output". Discuss.

Chapter Twelve

Economic Instability

Economic Instability

Key Terms

Economic instability, inflation, inflation rate, unemployment, consumer price index, unemployment rate

Usually *economic instability* is observed through trends in inflation and unemployment rate

Objectives

In this chapter, you will

❑ describe the causes of inflation

❑ provide possible remedies for inflation

❑ mention the uses of the consumer price index

❑ classify unemployment according to its causes

❑ describe possible remedies to reduce the rate of unemployment

12.1 Economists Can Observe Economic Instability

How do economists observe economic instability? Usually economic instability is observed through trends in inflation and unemployment rate. The aim of this chapter is to review the issue of **economic instability** by concentrating on the ways instability is revealed through inflation and unemployment rate.

12.2 Inflation

Inflation is a persistence rise in the general level of prices in an economy over a period of time. Inflation is a sustained rise in the general price level or a fall in the purchasing power of money.

Classification of Inflation

Inflation is classified according to degree of intensity, or according to its causes, or according to the sector of the economy.

Inflation according to *degree of intensity* (severity) may be classified as:

1. Creeping (or mild or gradual).
2. Walking (or trotting or moderate).
3. Running.
4. Hyperinflation (or runaway or galloping).

Thus, inflation according to degree of intensity ranges from gradual inflation up to runaway inflation.

Inflation according to *its causes* may be classified as:

1. Demand-pull (or excess demand).
2. Cost-push.
3. Structural (or demand shift).
4. Imported.
5. Expectation.
6. Monetary.

Thus, there may be many causes of inflation.

Inflation can also be classified according to the *sector of the economy*. Inflation according to the sector of the economy may be classified as underlying inflation and headline inflation.

12.3   Causes of Inflation

Generally the causes of inflation are of two categories namely demand-pull inflation and cost-push inflation.

Demand-Pull Inflation

Factors which cause inflation by increasing aggregate demand may include:
1. Increase in money supply.
2. Increase in disposable income.
3. Increase in public expenditure.
4. Increase in consumption.
5. Expansionary monetary policy.
6. Deficit financing.
7. Increase in investment.
8. Increase in underground economy.
9. Repayment of internal debt.
10. Export surplus.
11. Increase in population.

Cost-Push Inflation

Cost push inflation may arise from wage-push inflation and profit-push inflation. Factors which cause inflation by reducing aggregate supply may include:

1. Shortage of factors of production.
2. Presence of monopolies.
3. Power of trade unions.
4. Increase in exports.
5. Black marketing.
6. Deficit financing.
7. Production of luxuries.
8. Poor technology.
9. Saving schemes.
10. Reduction of imports.
11. Fiscal policy.
12. Reorganization of distributional channels of goods.
13. Prices and income policies.
14. Production policy.
15. Exchange rate policy.

12.4   The Problem of Inflation

Why is inflation regarded as undesirable in an economy? Although mild inflation may be healthy in an economy, people are regarding inflation to be undesirable. Inflation is regarded as undesirable for crucial reasons.   Possible reasons for undesirability of inflation are as follows:
1. Inflation causes social injustice.
2. Inflation may worsen the balance of payments.
3. Inflation results in creditors (lenders) losing money.
4. Inflation discourages business confidence.
5. Inflation may develop into hyperinflation.

12.5   Efforts to Reduce Inflation Rate

Anti-inflation policies depend on what is perceived to be the cause of inflation. There may be:

1. Remedies for demand-pull inflation. Such remedies may involve reducing government's fiscal budget deficit, reducing consumer demand, and tighter control over money supply.
2. Remedies for the monetarist view of inflation. That is, policies aimed at reducing the level of money in the economy.
3. Remedies for cost-push inflation. That is some kind of prices and incomes policy.

12.6   Consumer Price Index (CPI)

The **Consumer Price Index** (CPI) is a key economic indicator used by government, business, labour, academia, and other organizations to monitor price movements of a fixed basket of goods and services commonly purchased by households over a period of time.   Nonetheless, as time passes, consumption pattern change due to changes in consumer tastes, fashion, technology, and, most importantly, changes in the relative prices of the goods and services in the CPI market basket.   These changes cause the fixed basket of goods and services to become out of date and lead to an index that does not accurately reflect price change giving inaccurate market signal to index users. Hence, a need to review the CPI market basket from time to time.

Uses of the CPI

In Tanzania there are many uses of the CPI. For example:
1. The CPI is an indicator of price change. The CPI is the most common macro-economic indicator of price change. It is often used in the formulation of monetary policy and to identify the sources of price change.
2. The CPI is used for adjustment of economic series. The CPI is used as a price deflator in the compilation of real economic statistics and indicators, e.g., Gross Domestic Product (GDP) at constant prices.
3. The CPI is used for indexation of wages and salaries. Trade unions and employers use the CPI for the indexation of wages and salaries in order to maintain the purchasing power of the wages and salaries.
4. The CPI is used for international comparisons. The CPI is used to compare the inflation rate in Tanzania with that of other countries. The comparisons can be used to appraise the relative economic performance of Tanzania with that of other countries. This helps to determine socio-economic policy for the country.

12.7 Classifying Unemployment According to Causes

Classification of **unemployment** according to causes is as follows:
1. Frictional unemployment (also called normal or transitional or search).
2. Cyclical unemployment (also called inadequate-demand unemployment or Keynessian unemployment).
3. Seasonal unemployment.
4. Structural unemployment.

5. Technological unemployment.
6. Regional unemployment.

12.8   The Impact of Unemployment

Excessive unemployment may hurt the economy in several ways:
1. Unemployment reduces efficiency.
2. Unemployment hurts the least economically secure.
3. Unemployment damages worker's self-confidence.

12.9   Efforts to Reduce the Unemployment Rate

Possible efforts to reduce unemployment rate include:
1. The defeat of inflation.
2. The introduction training schemes to provide people the skills that will make their employment more likely.
3. Initiatives to promote the setting-up and growth of small firms.
4. Reduction in corporate taxes to stimulate growth in large firms and therefore stimulate the demand for labour.
5. Attempts to increase competition and de-regulate the markets.
6. Reductions in top rate personal taxes.

12.10 Key Employment Indicators

Key **employment indicators** are as follows:
1. Labour force. This is the total number of people of working age in work or actively seeking work.
2. Labour force participation rate. This is the labour force as a proportion of the total working age population.
3. Employment by industry sector. This is how many people work in agriculture and manufacturing industries, relative to services.
4. Employment status. This is the number of people employed full-time, part-time, or in temporary work.
5. Unemployment. This is the number of people registered as being without work, and as a proportion of the total labour force. This is the unemployment rate.

Review Questions

1. Describe the causes of inflation.
2. Provide possible remedies for inflation.
3. Mention the uses of the consumer price index.
4. Classify unemployment according to its causes.
5. Describe possible remedies to reduce the rate of unemployment.

Chapter Thirteen

The Central Bank and Monetary Policy

The Central Bank and Monetary Policy

Key Terms	Objectives
monetary policy, central bank, money supply, open market operations, bank rate, secondary reserve ratio, moral suasion	In this chapter, you will
	❑ understand the central bank as the apex of the banking system
Monetary policies are aimed at influencing the quantity of money, the price of money (interest rates), and the availability of credit in the economy	❑ revisit the functions of the Bank of Tanzania
	❑ understand the aims of monetary policies
	❑ describe the various ways of regulating the supply of money in an economy
	❑ distinguish between an easy and a tight monetary policy

13.1   Meaning of the Central Bank

The central bank is the apex of the banking system. The central bank is the hub of the banking system. The central bank is the heart of the banking system. The central bank is a national bank that does business with the government and other banks, and issues the country's coins and paper money.

Functions of the Central Bank

In Tanzania the **functions of a central bank** are as follows:
1. Banker to the government.
2. Note issue.
3. Banker to the banks.
4. Responsibility to the government debt.
5. Lender of last resort.
6. Bank supervision.
7. Implementation of monetary policy.

In Tanzania the **Bank of Tanzania** (BoT) performs the functions of the central bank. The BoT started its operations in 1966.

13.2   The Aims of Monetary Policies

Monetary policies are policies implemented by the treasury and the Bank of Tanzania (referred jointly as the monetary authorities) and are aimed at influencing the following:
1. The quantity of money.
2. The price of money (interest rates).
3. The availability of credit in the economy.

For instance, in times of recession when there is a widespread unemployment, a policy that stimulates the economy is appropriate. The Bank of Tanzania can act to increase the money supply to make it easier for banks to lend money, and for consumers, and provincial and local governments to borrow more money. This kind of action by the central bank is called an expansionary or easy money policy.

13.3   The World as Seen From the Central Bank

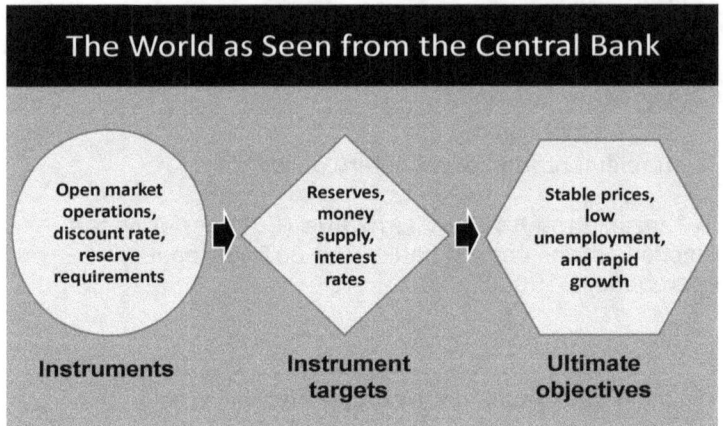

The World as Seen from the Central Bank

Open market operations, discount rate, reserve requirements

Instruments

Reserves, money supply, interest rates

Instrument targets

Stable prices, low unemployment, and rapid growth

Ultimate objectives

While the central bank ultimately pursues objectives like stable prices, its short term operations focus on the intermediate targets.

In determining monetary policy, the Central Bank manipulates the instruments or **policy variables** under its control.   The policy variables are open market operations, discount rate, and reserve requirements.

These policy variables help determine bank reserves, the money supply, and interest rates. Reserves, money supply, and interest rates are **instrument targets**.   Ultimately, monetary and fiscal policies are partners in pursuing the **major objectives** of rapid growth, low unemployment, and stable prices.

13.4 The Regulation of Money Supply in an Economy

There are various ways for regulation of money supply in an economy. The central bank may regulate the supply of money through the following ways:
1. Open market operations (OMO).
2. Changes in bank rate.
3. Changes in the secondary reserve ratio.
4. Moral suasion.

Open market operations are the purchase and sale of government bonds by the Bank of Tanzania to control the money supply. **Bank rate** is the rate of interest charged by the Bank of Tanzania on loans made to the commercial banks. The bank rate is trend-setting, effecting changes in the rates of interest that banks charge their customers. **Moral suasion** is an activity whereby the Bank of Tanzania tries to persuade commercial banks to vary their lending policies in the best interest of the country.

13.5 Increasing the Supply of Money in an Economy

Expansionary monetary policy is a plan to increase the money supply. Easy-money policy is another name for expansionary monetary policy. Monetary authorities may increase the supply of money in an economy through conducting an easy monetary policy. An illustration is provided below.

An Illustration of an Easy Monetary Policy

When the central bank wants to increase the supply of money in an economy it employs an **easy monetary policy**.

Easy monetary policy may include:

1. A participation in an open market operation through buying government securities and bonds; or
2. A reduction in the bank rate; or
3. A reduction in the secondary reserve ratio; or
4. Some combination of the above ways.

If an easy monetary policy is successful, then the supply of money in an economy increases. An easy monetary policy is also called an expansionary policy.

By buying government bonds the Bank of Tanzania can expand the money supply.

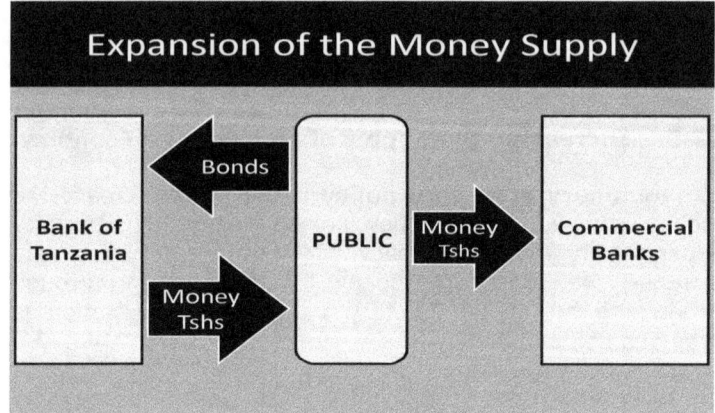

Open market operations influence the rate of interest. An increase in the money supply with a given demand for money will tend to force interest rates down.

If the Bank of Tanzania lowers the bank rate, then the commercial banks tend to lower theirs. Decreases in interest rates tend to encourage borrowing. Thus, in this way the Bank of Tanzania influence an increase in the supply of money.

The effect of all decreases in the secondary reserve ration (assuming the banks have no excess reserves) is to allow commercial banks to increase their loans and their deposits. Thus the money supply is increased.

13.6   Decreasing the Supply of Money in an Economy

Contractionary monetary policy is a plan to reduce the money supply. Tight-money policy is another name for contractionary monetary policy. Monetary authorities may decrease the supply of money in an economy through conducting a tight monetary policy. An illustration is provided below.

An Illustration of a Tight Monetary Policy

When the central bank wants to decrease the supply of money in an economy it employs a **tight monetary policy**. That policy may include:

1.   A participation in an open market operation through selling government securities and bonds; or
2.   An increase in the bank rate; or
3.   An increase in the secondary reserve ratio; or
4.   Some combination of the above ways.

If a tight monetary policy is successful, then the supply of money in an economy decreases. A tight money policy is also called a contraction policy.

By selling government bonds the Bank of Tanzania can contract the money supply.

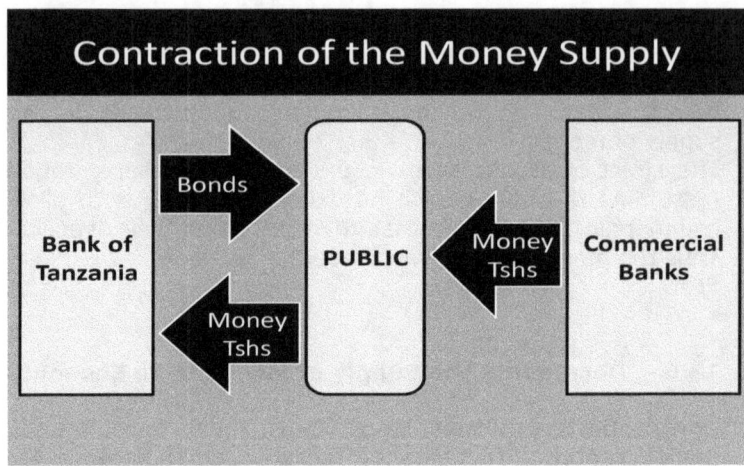

Open market operations influence the rate of interest. A decrease in the money supply with a given demand for money will tend to force interest rates up.

If the Bank of Tanzania raises the bank rate, then the commercial banks tend to raise theirs. Increases in interest rates tend to discourage borrowing. Thus, in this way the Bank of Tanzania influence a decrease in the supply of money.

The effect of all increases in the secondary reserve ratio (assuming the banks have no excess reserves) is to force commercial banks to diminish their loans and their deposits. Thus the money supply is diminished.

Review Questions

1. "The central bank is the apex of the banking system". Discuss.
2. Mention the functions of the Bank of Tanzania.
3. What are the aims of monetary policies?
4. Describe the various ways of regulating the supply of money in an economy.
5. Distinguish between an easy and a tight monetary policy.

Chapter Fourteen

International Trade

International Trade

Key Terms

International trade, open
  economy, closed economy,
  absolute advantage,
  comparative advantage,
  international specialization,
  free trade, protectionism,
  trade barriers, tariffs, terms
  of trade, balance of
  payments, exchange rates

International trade is trade
  between nations in goods
  and services

Objectives

In this chapter, you will

❏ understand a need for
  international trade

❏ state the law of comparative
  advantage

❏ provide arguments for and
  against free international
  trade

❏ illustrate the effects of tariffs
  to an economy

❏ define the balance of
  payments

14.1 A Need for International Trade

Few countries can produce everything they need
themselves. International trade occurs because, by
exchanging its own surplus goods and services for goods
and services produced by other countries, a country can
become better off.

International trade is trade between nations in goods and services. International trade is held to take place because of cost differences between nations or because of absolute non-availability of goods and services in countries. International trade leads to gains from trade.

The **theory of comparative advantage** shows that the difference required in costs between nations is not an absolute advantage but a comparative advantage, based on a difference in cost structure among countries. An **open economy** involves international trade, while a **closed economy** does not involve international trade. There is no country which is self-sufficient in everything. Therefore there is a need for international trade.

Differences between Domestic and International trade

Differences between domestic and international trade are as follows:
1. Within the domestic economy there is a general pattern of habits, customs, laws and attitudes towards production and consumption, but there are no similar patterns in the international economy.
2. There is a common currency within a country, but international trade involves a variety of currencies and rates of exchange.
3. There are few artificial barriers to the free flow of the factors of production within the domestic economy. But international trade is characterized by many such barriers, e.g., quotas and tariffs, and immigration controls.

Why Do Nations Trade?

Arguments for international trade which are the advantages of international specialization and trade include:

1. Each country can specialize in the production of the goods which it is best capable of producing, and, thus, the world's resources are utilized more effectively.
2. Large scale production for wide markets and the resultant economies of scale are encouraged.
3. Countries are able to obtain a wide range of commodities, and standards of living are raised.
4. Local deficiencies in supply can be remedied where there is access to international sources of supply.
5. International specialization tends to maximize world output.
6. International trade serves as a means of developing political links with other countries.
7. International trade increases competition and possible efficiency of production.

Absolute Advantage

A country is said to have an **absolute advantage** in the production of a commodity if it can produce that commodity more efficiently. This means that production in this country yields more output for a given level of inputs.

Comparative Advantage

The law (theory) of **comparative advantage** is an explanation of why international trade can be beneficial for all the countries that engage in it. It was developed by David Ricardo an English economist, in the 19th century. A country has a comparative advantage over another country in producing a particular good, if, before it establishes trade with the other country, its cost of production for that good is low, not only compared to its cost of producing some other good, but also compared to the relative production costs of the two goods in the other country. The theory of comparative (or relative) advantage shows that relative costs are important in determining which products are imported and exported.

A country will export a product for which it has relatively low production costs, and will import a product for which it has relatively high production costs. Mutually advantageous trades can always take place between two countries or regions whose pretrade price structures differ.

An Illustration of the Law of Comparative Advantage

Let us look at the following illustration of the **law of comparative advantage**.

Let us assume that we have two countries, namely *Freeland* and *Bongoland*. With no specialization, one day's labour in *Freeland* results in 40 tons of cassava and 80 tons of maize. *Freeland's* opportunity cost for 1 ton of cassava is 2 tons of maize. While with no specialization, one day's labour in *Bongoland* results in 50 tons of cassava and 200 tons of maize. *Bongoland's* opportunity cost for 1 ton of cassava is 4 tons of maize.

With specialization and trade, *Freeland* trades 1 ton of cassava and gets 3 tons of maize from *Bongoland*. The **benefit of trade** is as follows; it used to cost *Freeland* 1 ton of cassava to get 2 tons of maize: now it trades 1 ton of cassava for 3 tons of maize.

At the same time, with specialization and trade *Bongoland* trades 3 tons of maize and gets 1 ton of cassava from *Freeland*. The **benefit of trade** is as follows: it used to cost *Bongoland* 4 tons of maize for 1 ton of cassava; now it trades only 3 tons of maize for 1 ton of cassava.

14.2   Meaning of a Free International Trade

Free international trade is a free international policy of non-intervention by the state in trade between nations, where trade takes place according to the international division of labour and the theory of comparative advantage. Such a policy would lead to the most efficient allocation of resources on a world scale and to the maximization of world income.

Arguments for Free International Trade

Arguments for free international trade, which are the advantages obtained if there is trade without hindrance, include:
1. Output as a whole is undertaken efficiently and at least cost.
2. Countries obtain goods which are otherwise unobtainable.
3. World output is increased (production will be maximized).
4. Specialization leads to economies of scale.

5. Unrestricted free trade will allow every nation to concentrate on the type of production for which it is best fitted, and this will increase the world's total wealth.
6. Prices are cheaper under free trade than they would be if international specialization were restricted.
7. Home producers are stimulated to greater effort by the spur of international competition.
8. A wider range of choices is available to consumers.

14.3   Barriers to International Trade

Despite the strong theoretical backing for free trade, free trade has rarely if ever been practiced by one country let alone by the community of all countries. Governments may intervene in international trade for non-economic reasons (e.g., for national defense or for social reasons) or economic reasons (e.g., protection of established industries from imports, the protection of infant industries, the terms of trade argument, and the cheap labour argument).

Protectionism is the use of trade barriers between nations to protect domestic industries.

Barriers to international trade include:

1) **Trade barriers** (A trade barrier is any law that limits free trade between nations)
   a) Tariffs (A tariff is a fee charged for goods brought into one country from another)
      i) **Revenue tariffs** (A revenue tariff is a tax levied on imports specifically to raise money). Revenue tariff is not a protective measure.
      ii) **Protective tariffs** (A protective tariff is a tax on imported goods to protect domestic goods).

b) **Embargoes** (An embargo is a law that cuts off trade with a specific country).
c) **Quotas** (A quota is a limit the amount of the product that can be imported).
d) **Voluntary export restraint** (VER) (A voluntary export restraint is a country's self-imposed restriction on exports).
e) **Subsidies** or bounties (Subsidies results into a reduction of imports).
f) **Exchange control** (foreign currency is not made available to pay for imports).
g) Government action to **depreciate the currency** (reduces its foreign exchange value).

2) **Informal trade barriers**
a) Licenses.
b) Environmental regulations.
c) Health and safety measures.

Arguments against Free International Trade

Arguments against free international trade, which are the **arguments for protection** (i.e., trade restrictions) include:
1. Infant industry argument. That is, there is a need to restrict free international trade so as to protecting infant domestic industries.
2. Key defense industry argument. That is, there are some key industries that have to be protected as a way of protecting national security.
3. Employment argument. That is, protectionism helps in protecting domestic jobs.

4. Government revenue argument. That is, protectionism helps to increase government revenue.
5. Balance of payments argument. That is, restrictions may lead to correction of adverse balance of payments.
6. Protectionism may be a measure to counter 'dumping' of surplus production by other countries at an uneconomically low price.
7. Protectionism measures may be implemented in retaliation against measures taken by another country that are thought to be unfair.

Illustrations of Protective Tariffs

A trade restriction is any government measure that limits the free flow of trade. Its effect is to change the domestic price of imports or exports from the level that would be established by free trade in international markets. If a government restricts international trade the result will typically be an increase in that country's domestic market prices over international prices and a general reduction in the total economic welfare of that country and of the world.

Production, consumption, and revenue effects of a tariff can be illustrated by the following diagram.

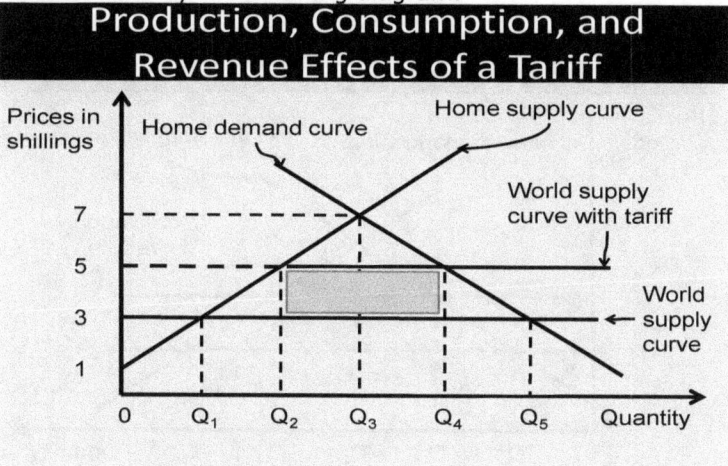

The above effects are as follows:
1. Price effect. The price of imports increases from 3 to 5.
2. Production effect on domestic production. Increase in domestic supply of goods from Q_1 units to Q_2 units.
3. Reduction in the demand for imports. The demand for imports decreases from (Q_5 minus Q_1) units to (Q_4 minus Q_2 units).
4. Consumption effects. Amount of consumption decreases by (Q_5 minus Q_4) units.
5. Revenue effect. Government receives a revenue which is equal to amount of imports times the per unit tax, that is, (Q_4 minus Q_2) times (5 minus 3) which is that area of the shaded rectangle.
6. Welfare effect. The welfare of consumers falls because they will be buying imports at higher prices and possibly buy low quality domestic goods. *(See details in the diagram below).*

Revenue, redistribution, and welfare effects of a tariff can be illustrated by the following diagram.

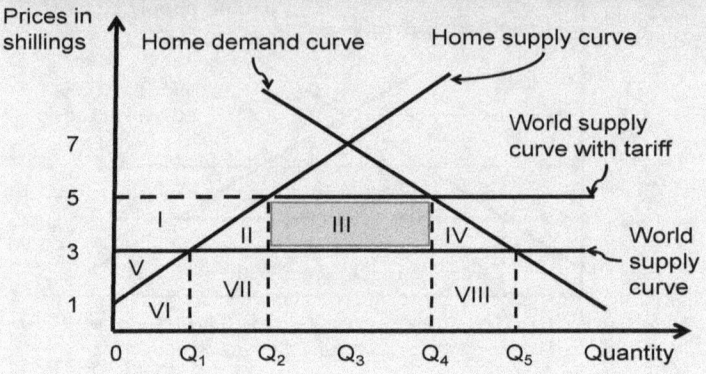

Revenue, Redistribution, and Welfare Effects of a Tariff

The above effects are as follows:
1. Revenue effect of tariff. Tariffs have the effect of directly increasing the revenue of the government of the country that levies them. In the figure above Government receives revenue which is equal to area III.
2. Redistribution effect of tariff. Area I represents the increase in domestic producer's surplus. Although consumers have been hurt, domestic producers have benefited from the tariff.
3. Consumers are deprived of area I + II + III + IV. Part of this lost surplus is area III which has gone to the government as revenue, and area I which has gone to domestic producers.
4. The loss in consumer welfare. That is area IV + VIII.

5. The production cost of tariff. That is triangle II which is due to misallocation of resources into inefficient production because of the tariff.
6. The consumption cost of protection. That is triangle IV.
7. Deadweight losses. The deadweight loses are area II and IV which are the cost of tariff to society. That is, nobody in the society receives the amount which is in those two triangles.

However, as long as there are unemployed resources in the economy, tariffs may cause an increase in welfare because they enable import-competing industries to expand production and employment. But, there is a danger of retaliation from foreign governments which may cause unemployment in our export industries, thereby lowering our welfare.

14.4   The Terms of Trade

The ratio at which a country's exports exchange for imports is known as the country's **terms of trade**. A rise in terms of trade is interpreted as favourable, while a fall is interpreted as unfavourable.

14.5   The Balance of Payments

The **balance of payments** is a record of a country's international transactions, monetary and commercial. The balance of payments is a record of all the transactions that occurred between the individuals, businesses, government units of one nation and those of the rest of the world.
The three sections of the balance are:
1. The current account.
2. Investment and other capital flows.
3. Official financing.

Balance of Payments Deficits and Surpluses

A nation's **balance of trade** is the difference between the value of its imports and exports. A nation with a trade surplus exports more than it imports. A nation with a trade deficit imports more than it exports.

As mentioned above, the **balance of payments** is a record of all transactions that occurred between the individuals, businesses, and government units of one nation and those of the rest of the world. Balance of payments deficit occurs whenever a country pays more than what it receives; while a balance of payments surplus occurs whenever a country receives more than what it pays.

Contents of the Balance of Payments

The Britain's balance of payments for 1973 is used as an illustration for the concepts related to the balance of payments.
Contents of the table are as follows:

- **Exports** are goods and services produced in one country (Britain in the table above) and sold to other countries (the rest of the world).
- **Imports** are goods and services produced in one country (the rest of the world) and purchased by another (Britain in the table above).
- The **visible trade balance** (balance of trade) is the difference between the value of goods exported and imported.
- "**Invisible transactions**" include expenditure and receipts concerning government expenditure abroad, shipping and civil aviation, insurance and banking services, travel, interest, profits and dividends, and private transfers (migrants' remittances, etc.).
- **Current balance** ("balance of payment on current account") is the visible and invisible balances taken together.

Britain's Balance of Payments for 1973	
	Million Pounds
Exports	11435
Imports	13810
Visible balance	**2375**
Government services and transfers (net)	-790
Other invisibles	
Private services and transfers (net)	+860
Interest, profits, dividends (net)	
Private sector	+1290
Public sector	-195
Invisible balance	**+1165**
Current balance	**-1210**
Total investment and other capital flows	+1071
Balancing item	+408
Total currency flow	**+210**
Official financing:	
Official reserves	-210
Total official financing	**-210**

- The **total currency flow** records official and private overseas investments and foreign investments etc., in the country.
- The **balancing item** is necessary to balance the accounts, and represents errors and omissions I other items.

The **official financing item** records changes in country's foreign currency reserves.

The balance of payments *always balances*. What is of significance is *how* the two sides of the account are balanced.

Measures to Correct a Balance of Payments Deficit

An adverse balance of payments on current account may be caused by the following factors:
1. Adverse terms of trade.
2. Exports may be over-priced because domestic industry is inefficient compared with foreign industry.
3. An adverse balance on the capital account.

Remedies for deficits on the balance of payments can be temporal measure or other measures which deal with the fundamental causes of the deficit.

Temporary measures include the following:
1. Borrowing from International Monetary Fund.
2. Selling foreign assets.
3. Obtaining loans from abroad.
4. Drawing on gold and currency reserves.

Other measures which deal with the fundamental causes of the deficit include the following:

1. Restrictions on imports, government expenditure and abroad investments. Tariffs, quotas, subsidies and exchange controls may be used.
2. Deflation leading to a fall in the level of prices may be used. This action would, in theory, raise the relative price of imports and lower the price of exports. Deflation is characterized by a situation in which there is a deliberate contraction in the supply of money to spend relative to the available supply of goods and services.
3. Devaluation may be used. Devaluation results from a government decision to reduce the value of the country's currency relative to gold or to the currency of other countries.

   In theory, devaluation should be followed immediately by an expansion of exports and a decrease in imports. In practice, the effect of devaluation depends on the elasticities of demand and supply in relation to exports and imports, the possibilities of retaliation by other major trading countries and the fear of further devaluation and its effect on confidence in the devalued currency.

14.6 Exchange Rates

Foreign exchange is the system of exchanging the money of one country for that of another country. In the **foreign exchange market**, the currencies of different countries are bought and sold. The **foreign exchange rate** is the price of a currency in the currencies of other nations.

With a **fixed exchange rate**, the currency of one nation is fixed, or constant, in relation to other currencies. The **flexible rate of exchange** is a system in which the exchange rate for currency changes as supply and demand for the currency changes.

14.7   The Aims of the International Monetary Fund

The **International Monetary Fund** (IMF) was established by the Bretton Woods agreement in 1946. The three broad aims of the International Monetary Fund are:
1. To promote international monetary co-operation, and to establish a code of conduct for making international payments.
2. To provide financial support to countries with temporary balance of payments deficits.
3. To provide for the orderly growth of international liquidity.

The IMF is the organization within the United Nations which is concerned with trade and economic development. The United Nations is an association of many countries which aims to improve economic and social conditions and to solve political problems in the world in a peaceful way.

Review Questions

1. Why do nations need international trade?
2. "The law of comparative advantage is a foundation for international trade". Discuss.
3. Provide arguments for free international trade.
4. Provide arguments against free international trade.
5. Illustrate the effects of tariffs to an economy.
6. Describe the balance of payments as a record of a country's international transactions.
7. What is a foreign exchange market?
8. Mention three broad aims of the International Monetary Fund.

Chapter Fifteen

Economic Integration

Economic Integration

Key Terms	Objectives
economic integration, forms of integration, preferential trade area, free trade area, customs union, common market, economic union, trade creation, trade diversion	In this chapter, you will
	❏ classify forms of integration according to level of development
	❏ identify conditions necessary for success of economic integration
A customs union is an agreement that abolishes trade barriers among its members and establishes uniform tariffs for non-members	❏ Indicate the advantages and disadvantages of economic integration
	❏ identify the East African Community as an example of economic integration

15.1 Forms of Integration (Types of Integration)
Economic integration can be classified according to its level of development as follows:
1. Preferential trade area.
2. Free trade area.
3. Customs union.
4. Common market.
5. Economic community (union).

A **preferential trade area** is the lowest level of economic integration, while economic union is the highest level of economic integration. In the preferential trade area there is a reduction of tariffs among members.

A **free trade area** is specific region in which trade between nations take place without protective tariffs.

A **customs union** is an arrangement that abolishes trade barriers among its members and establishes uniform tariffs for non members. A customs union is free trade area *plus* common external tariffs.

A **common market** is a customs union *plus* free movement of factors of production.

An **economic union** is a common market *plus* common currency.

15.2   Conditions for Success of Economic Integration

Some of the conditions necessary for success of economic integration include:
1.   Geographical proximity.
2.   Equal stages of development.
3.   Same ideology.
4.   More or less equal size.
5.   Commitment of member states.

15.3   Advantages of Economic Integration

Possible **advantages of economic integration** include:
1.   Trade creation effects.
2.   Increases in market size.

3. Rational location of industries.
4. Reduction in costs of reduplication.
5. Easy access to foreign resources.
6. Jointly access to research and development activities.
7. Increases in variety of commodities produced and consumed.
8. Reduction in the costs of production.
9. Improvement on the quality of products.
10. Increases in the bargaining power.
11. A sharing in the common services.
12. Possibility of a common currency.
13. Free movement of factors of production.
14. Political cooperation and enhancement of peace and stability.
15. Availability of commodities.

The advantages depend on the level of integration and commitment of member states.

15.4   Disadvantages of Economic Integration

Some of the **disadvantages of economic integration** include:
1. Trade diversion.
2. Balance of payments problems.
3. Poor quality goods.
4. Uneven distribution of industries.
5. Weak commitment.
6. Competition and unemployment.
7. Difficulties in harmonizing external tariffs.
8. Political problems.
9. Unreliable transport and communication.
10. Language differences.
11. Reliance on the production and export of raw materials.
12. Loss of revenue due to removal of tariffs.

13. Production of the same commodities.
14. Shortage of funds to finance integration.

15.5   Countries of the East African Community

The **East African Community** is an example of economic integration.   Its member states, arranged according to geographical sizes, as at year 2012 are as follows:
1.   Tanzania.
2.   Kenya.
3.   Uganda.
4.   Burundi.
5.   Rwanda.

Review Questions

1.   Provide a classification of forms of integration according to level of integration.
2.   Mention conditions necessary for success of economic integration.
3.   What are the possible advantages of economic integration?
4.   What are the possible disadvantages of economic integration?
5.   Mention member states that belong to the East African Community.

Index